D0674092

the home
advisor

the home
advisor

HUMAN & ROUSSEAU
Cape Town Pretoria Johannesburg

ROD BAKER

THANK YOU TO
Burkhard Grensemann of Robert Bosch SA (Pty) Ltd,
for the tools used in photographs throughout the book

Ron van Til of Central Mica Hardware (Pty) Ltd, Fish Hoek,
for photographic props used in the book

PHOTOGRAPHIC CREDITS

Ryno: pp. 1, 2/3, 4, 6, 9, 10, 12, 16, 29, 30, 35, 45, 48, 53, 69, 74, 77, 87, 88, 93, 99, 103, 105, 111, 113, 119, 125, 126, 131, 146, and top photo on back cover
Dook: pp. 52, 143   **Adriaan Oosthuizen:** p. 117

All interior photographs from VISI; copyright strictly reserved
DIY photographs supplied by author

Copyright © 2002 by Rod Baker
First published in 2002 by Human & Rousseau,
28 Wale Street, Cape Town
Typography and cover design by Tracey Mackenzie
Background photograph on cover: Image Bank
All illustrations except page 136 by Fiona Young
Illustration on page 136 by Gusti Prohn
Text electronically prepared and typeset in 11 on 13 pt Stone Sans
by ALINEA STUDIO, Cape Town
Colour separation by Virtual Colour
Printed and bound through Colorcraft, Hong Kong

ISBN 0 7981 4232 4

contents

introduction

There's nothing quite like the satisfaction of a job well done – especially when you never thought you could do it in the first place. And when you try, you will be amazed at how many things you can do.

And that applies to both men and women. One used to think that the man of the house put up the shelves and serviced the car, while the woman of the house cooked and took care of the VCR remote (ever noticed how women are better at setting up the VCR to record than men are?). Well, that's all changed – now the ladies will be able to cook, work the remote – and work on the car!

This book has been designed to whet your appetite. It doesn't set out to be the complete answer to everything that you will ever face, but what I have tried to do is provide you with a wealth of hints, tips and ideas to help you on your way. For instance, the hint on shoe storage does not provide precise construction details because this book is not about projects; I want to suggest ideas for you to adopt – and adapt – to suit your particular situation.

I have begun with what I believe is the most important aspect, however: looking after yourself and your loved ones. After all, pain and suffering is not meant to be a part of working around the home.

But the fact is, many if not most accidents do occur in and around the home, so the first aim is to do things safely – and Be Prepared!

From there I go into the General section (which is just that – very general), containing the basics of electrical work, basic plumbing, running repairs on your car, basic wood joins and painting tips – plus a lot more.

I cannot stress enough, however, that when doing electrical work you should not attempt anything beyond your skills or knowledge. Rather call the experts.

The last two main sections cover the home and the garden respectively. In the Home section you will find hints on general home maintenance and decorating, plus simple furniture repairs and a host of other subjects.

The Garden section covers everything from braais to birds, walls to water . . . even poisonous plants and using plants to hide that ugly shed. They're all there, plus more.

Finally, as I stress throughout: call the experts – but it's not much use if you have to wade through the Internet and the Yellow Pages to find the information you need. So I've done it for you (well, a lot of it, anyway): I've provided you with a pretty comprehensive list of useful contacts – and even some space for you to add your own.

Enjoy yourself – but be careful.

Rod Baker

be prepared

There is only one thing worse than taking two precautions too many, and that's taking one too few. And let's face it, once you're on your way down the roof, or the ladder has toppled with you on it, it's too late to say 'I should just have . . .'

If an injury does occur, being well prepared will be of great help. Although not intended to be a complete guide to every injury that can occur in the home, this section covers what we think are the more common injuries or conditions. The main point, however, is this: when in the slightest doubt, get the victim medical attention as soon as possible.

Previous page: *Be sure to place upholstered furniture at a safe distance from an open fireplace, not only to avoid damage caused by flying embers, but also as a safeguard against fire (see p. 11).*
This page: *Most accidents occur in and around the home. A fall from a ladder can lead to sprains, fractures or even concussion (see p. 19), so do take care!*

BASIC SAFETY

PUT THAT FIRE OUT!
A carelessly discarded match, a glowing ember from a fireplace, an electrical short . . . there are many causes of fire in the home and workshop, and a little knowledge of how to put one out is invaluable.

- Do not use water on an electrical fire. Turn off the power source and smother the flames using a dry powder extinguisher or fire blanket. Aim the extinguisher at the base of the fire.
- If fuel or paint has caught alight, do not use water either: petrol, for instance, floats on water and all you will do is spread the fire. Use a fire blanket or a dry powder extinguisher, aimed at the base of the fire, to smother the flames.
- When frying foods or cooking with fat, keep a large pot lid handy – one that will completely cover the pan or pot you are using. If the fat catches fire, drop the lid onto the cooking utensil – deprived of oxygen, the fire will be extinguished.

CHOOSING A FIRE EXTINGUISHER
- A dry powder extinguisher is suitable for use on flammable liquids, paper, wood and textiles, as well as electrical fires, and these cover most of what you are likely to encounter in the home and garage.
- Rather than buying a single large appliance, purchase two smaller ones of, say, 1,5 kg capacity. They are light, portable and handy, and if you have two, you double your chances of being able to get to one in an emergency. Mount them on a wall, at a convenient height, at the entrance to your garage and in your kitchen.
- A very useful item in addition to an extinguisher is a fire blanket – consider buying one of these as well. It is simply dropped onto the fire, smothering the flames.

SIMPLE FIRE PRECAUTIONS
- Keep matches and lighters out of the reach of children.
- Make sure that blankets and upholstered furniture are placed away from an open fireplace.
- If you use a bar heater in the home, ensure that blankets, clothing and flammable items such as magazines are kept well away from it.
- In the garage, store paints, varnishes, solvents and other flammable substances on a platform on which you have mounted casters – if a fire breaks out, you will be able to move everything out in a moment. Position the platform near the garage door, so that you're as close to an exit as possible.
- Keep the garage clean and clear of debris such as wood shavings. You might later be using an angle grinder on metal and the sparks could ignite the shavings, which could smoulder for hours before flaring up in that patch of oil you didn't clean up!

A good, general-purpose extinguisher, available from hardware stores, is a very useful item to have in the home.

A platform on casters is a simple means to get your flammable items out of the workshop or garage in a hurry. We've got gas bottles and paints on the same trolley to illustrate the point but, for safety, you might prefer to make up a couple of trolleys, each for a specific purpose.

Besides being fast and efficient, gas stoves are also potentially dangerous and the necessary fire precautions need to be taken at all times (see p. 11). Working with a stove and boiling substances can often lead to burns which need immediate and proper treatment (see p. 18).

A prominent notice stuck over the relevant switch is a good warning to others.

ELECTRIC SHOCK – DON'T LET THE FORCE BE WITH YOU

Electrical power is great when used properly and treated with respect, but accidents can occur when something you thought was off, is actually on. You open the cover, and . . .

So this is a case where two precautions too many are much better than one too few:

- Always switch off the power and unplug any appliance before dismantling it.
- Always ensure that everyone else in the house knows what you're doing and will not plug in the appliance or turn on the mains power, if you have turned it off for a particular reason.
- Stick a big notice on the relevant switch, telling everyone to leave it alone.
- Switch on a TV or radio and turn the volume right up. You won't hear anything if no one switches on the power, but if they do, you will – and the split-second warning could save your life.

POWER TOOL SAFETY

Power tools are one of humankind's better inventions, but anything that can cut, shape, or make holes in wood, metal and other materials will make short work of your flesh. And very quickly too!

However, a few simple rules will keep your flesh safe and ensure that your fondness for power tools never diminishes:

- Use the tool for the purpose for which it was intended.
- Keep a tight grip on it while in use – use both hands if that is what the manufacturer recommends.
- Keep the work area clear.
- Wear the necessary protective gear.
- Do not use a power tool if you have consumed any alcohol or taken any medication that might affect your concentration.
- Concentrate on what you're doing.
- Do not be distracted by children or anyone else. But if it happens, turn off the power tool before responding.
- Work away from the cord.
- Ensure you have a proper stance before starting a particular task – if you overbalance you could injure yourself.
- Do not wear loose clothing and tie long hair back – if it gets caught you could end up more closely involved in the task than you want to be.
- Turn off and unplug the tool before changing any blade, bit or accessory. If you leave it plugged in, you might accidentally start it up.
- If you smell that particular 'electrical' smell when using a power tool, turn it off and check that everything is in order. If it is simply running hot, run it at full speed under no load – its cooling fan will cool it faster than if you left it on the bench to cool.
- Don't mess about with the safety features of any power tool, such as a guard. Leave it in place, and do not adapt it to keep it clear of the workpiece.
- Don't use power tools outdoors in the rain, or indoors while you're standing in a wet patch on the floor.
- Ensure the workpiece is firmly anchored to a sturdy base – suddenly having the piece of material you're working on fly off the bench can result in injury.
- Should the workpiece fall despite your best efforts to secure it, let it do so – don't try to stop it with one hand while operating the tool with the other. You could injure yourself.

Always work away from the cord, not towards it.

Never tie a guard back; you're playing with fire – and the possibility of severe injury.

PESTICIDES – DEADLY IN THE WRONG HANDS

Pesticides, given the job they are intended to do, can be deadly, so treat them with caution:

- Use only as directed and ensure that pets are kept away from treated areas if you are using a pesticide that can harm animals.
- If you have to mix up an amount and have some left over, do not store it in a cool-drink bottle. If a child is able to reach it and is thirsty, they may try to drink it. The golden rule in any event is to keep all pesticides locked up and out of reach of young children.
- One further point: if you use a container such as a bucket for mixing pesticides or garden chemicals, mark it clearly so that you use only that container, and to ensure that it is not used for any other purpose. Even a tiny residue of a pesticide could be deadly if it finds its way into your pet's drinking water, for instance.

CUT THE GRASS – NOT YOUR TOES!

Lawnmowers are marvellous – but you have to treat them with respect. There are a couple of rules you should follow if you are to survive uninjured:

- First of all, never turn the mower on its side to remove an overload of cuttings, or whatever, while the power is still on. Turn it off and wait until the blades have come to a complete rest before investigating the problem. This is particularly important when using an electric mower, as some types take a few seconds to come to a standstill.
- If using a petrol-powered mower, pull the lead off the spark plug before clearing the blades – turning them while the engine is still hot and with the lead connected, could result in the motor starting up.
- Never use an electric mower in the rain or while the lawn is still damp from early-morning dew – if there is a fault in the wiring, you might never have to mow a lawn again. And a small tip: work away from the cord – cutting through one tends to put a damper on your day.
- Mower switches are designed to be 'on' under positive pressure from the user's hand. This is a safety precaution. So, if the switch develops a fault, **do not** bypass it – have it replaced.
- Push the mower away from you; never pull it towards yourself. When using an edge trimmer, work away from the cord by keeping it behind you and ensure it doesn't snag on anything. And wear stout shoes – your toes are fine just the way they are.

STAYING SAFE ON THE ROOF

A sloped roof is a dangerous place to work, so tie yourself up there. Take a length of strong rope – strong enough to support your weight – and tie one end to a stout anchor, for instance a large tree or veranda column, on the opposite side of the house to the one on which you're working.

A few simple precautions will keep you safe on your roof.

Fling the other end over the roof and once you're up there, tie the rope around your waist so that even if you do slip, you won't fall to the ground and injure yourself.

But some words of caution:

- **Do not** tie the end of the rope to any vehicle – your partner could forget where you are and decide to go shopping. It might sound amusing, but it has happened.
- **Do not** get on the roof if it looks like lightning. If lightning does strike, you might be the path – and dead or injured as a result. Incidentally, if lightning is about and your hair stands on end (as a result of static electricity), you are in great danger. Get down and under cover immediately.
- **Do not** wear loose-fitting footwear or shoes with soles that do not grip well. Wear footwear that fastens securely and has soles of rubber or a similar substance that gives your feet a good purchase on the roofing material, be it tiles, corrugated iron or whatever.
- **Do not** step just anywhere on a roof. Certain roofing materials might not take an adult's weight in an unsupported area. Place your weight where it will be supported by the timbers below the roofing material.
- **Warn** others to stay out of the way directly below where you're working. You might drop a tool, which could cause an injury if it hits anyone.

MIND YOUR TOES
A large sheet of plywood or a similar material might not be very heavy, but it can be awkward for one person to carry (and will feel heavy if the edge lands on your toes). Make up a loop of rope of sufficient length and loop it around the sheet's lower corners as shown. Now you can carry the sheet with ease.

A SHATTERING EXPERIENCE
When you need to remove a broken windowpane which is in a number of pieces, apply a few lengths of duct tape to it before starting. It will keep the pieces together so that they won't fall and shatter even more when they hit the ground.

YOU'VE GOT IT, SO LOOK AFTER IT!
Fumes, dust particles, loud noise, flying fragments . . . all of these can cause major health problems. And the remedy is so simple – wear protective gear!

There is a wide range of accessories that will protect your respiratory system, ears, eyes and skin from injury. When working with materials that give off fumes or dust, ensure that you have the correct filter in the mask, and when in doubt, check.

And go for quality – even the most expensive pair of goggles to protect your eyes when using an angle grinder, or muffs to protect your hearing when routing, are far cheaper than the medical bills you would have to pay in the event of a problem.

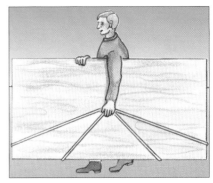

Loop the loop – and carry that large sheet without crushing your toes.

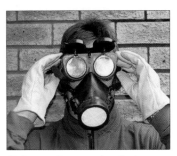

Take me to your leader! Rather overdoing it – but you'll need some or all of this protection for some jobs.

Sharp knives are essential kitchen tools, but they can also inflict nasty cuts. The correct treatment (see p. 17) will help prevent infection and, in the worst-case scenario, might save a life.

ESSENTIAL FIRST AID

ABRASIONS AND CUTS

A cut or abrasion can be trifling, or terrible – it depends on what caused it and the amount of force involved.

- Wash a minor wound under running water, treat it with a mild antiseptic and cover it with a plaster or gauze pad. Tissue paper will quickly absorb any moisture on the skin surrounding the wound and allow a plaster to adhere to the skin, but be careful not to touch the wound itself – you don't want any tissue fibres getting into it.
- If the wound is such that bleeding is severe, your main task is to control that first. If the injury is to a limb, raise it above chest level to reduce the pressure of the blood flow and use a gauze pad to apply firm pressure directly onto the wound. This flattens the blood vessels, slows the blood flow and allows more time for clots to form. If blood soaks through the pad, do not remove it, but place another pad on top of it and continue applying pressure until the bleeding stops or medical assistance is available.

BEAT THOSE BLISTERS

Generally, the blisters you are most likely to suffer in the home are due to burns, friction, a reaction to a plant, an insect bite or sting or, in the case of a blood blister, bad aim when using a tool such as a hammer.

Burns can occur in the kitchen, around the braai or just about anywhere. Friction blisters usually result when we decide to dig a new flowerbed and we haven't picked up a spade in months!

First rule – don't burst a blister unless the pressure of the fluid is causing discomfort. If you do puncture it, cover it with a light gauze pad to keep grime out, but allow it to 'breathe'. If it becomes infected, get medical attention.

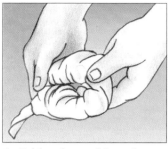

1. Fold a sheet of linen into a narrow strip, or use a narrow bandage. Wrap this loosely around your hand a few times, and then start passing the end around the loop you have made.

2. Once you have completed the ring, which should be reasonably firm, place it over the injury, taking care not to disturb the object in the wound.

3. Fix the ring in position with a roller bandage. Ensure that you do not tie the bandage over the object, pushing it further into the wound.

BURNS – THE DO'S AND DON'TS

Burns range in severity from minor to serious to life-threatening, depending on their size, situation and depth. Unless they are clearly minor, your doctor should see burns and scalds as they could be more serious than you first thought.

So . . .

- If the burn is due to a chemical spillage, use a soft brush to remove as much as you can and get the victim out of any clothing that has been contaminated by the chemical. Then hold the burned area under a slowly running cold-water tap for about 10 minutes to wash off the rest of the chemical.
- In the case of a heat burn, remove the victim from the source of the heat and hold the burned area under a slowly running cold-water tap for a few minutes. The aim is to bring the temperature of the skin down as soon as possible.
- **Do not** apply fat, butter, margarine, lotion or any other substance to the wound area. Do not burst any blister, remove any loose skin or interfere with the burn area at all.
- Remove any ring, watch or other item of jewellery and loosen any tight clothing near the site of the burn, in case any swelling develops. If a ring cannot be slipped off, cut it with sidecutters – it can be repaired.
- Treat any burn other than one that is clearly minor, as serious – and do not assume that the absence of pain means the burn is minor. If the skin is grey, charred or peeling, the nerves have probably been damaged and the burn is serious. Do not run cold water over this sort of burn.
- The bottom line is: when in any doubt, seek medical attention immediately.

PENETRATING WOUNDS

The first impulse when someone suffers a penetrating wound is to pull out the object – say a shard of glass – causing the damage. Don't do this! It might have severed a major blood vessel and removing it will cause severe bleeding.

The correct thing to do is to make up a ring bandage, as shown, and to place it over the wound. Then use a bandage to hold it firmly in position. The objective is to prevent any movement of the object in the wound, as even a slight movement could make the injury more serious. Then get the patient to medical attention.

SPRAINS AND FRACTURES

A sprain occurs when the ligaments around a joint are suddenly stretched or torn. Signs are pain, tenderness and swelling around a joint.

- Make the victim as comfortable as possible and raise the injured limb.
- Apply a cold compress to the joint, winding the bandage around the joint, snugly, but not too tightly, to help support it in one position.

A fracture is a partial or complete breakage of a bone and is far more serious. The victim might have heard or felt a bone break, there may be a deformity of the limb in the region of the fracture, swelling and, later, bruising, pain, tenderness and an inability to move the limb properly, if at all.

- **Do not** move the injured limb or part of the body unnecessarily. Support the limb by hand or by tying a splint to it, putting pads between the splint and any parts of a limb where a bone would be pressed hard against the hard material of the splint, for example the knee.
- Get the victim medical attention, and ensure that the fractured limb is supported during the trip to prevent any unnecessary movement.

CONCUSSION

Many tasks around the home and garden require you to mount ladders and chairs – and one slip can end up with you suffering concussion. And you won't necessarily pass out.

- Signs to look for in the unconscious victim are shallow breathing, a weak but rapid pulse, pale skin tone, and skin that is cold and clammy to the touch.
- A conscious victim, or one who has regained consciousness, might feel nauseous or already be vomiting, and might also be unable to remember what happened immediately prior to the incident. If he is unable to answer simple questions such as the date or time, concussion is probably the cause.
- Seek medical attention, as a more serious condition called compression could develop.

HINT

When working on the outside of a house, particularly a double-storey home, tie the top of the ladder to a roof truss before you start working. Even if there is some rope between the truss and the anchor point, the ladder won't fall, and should you slip, it will give you a chance of regaining your foothold.

BANDAGING WOUNDS

Generally, injuries around the home involve cuts, bruises, sprains, fractures and, less commonly, penetrating wounds. The golden rule in all these instances is not to apply the bandages too tightly.

Bandages are applied for any one reason, or a combination of reasons. For instance, it may be necessary to support a limb, apply pressure to a wound to slow or prevent bleeding, hold a limb in the same position, hold a splint in position, or prevent dirt entering a wound.

Ensure your home first-aid kit includes a variety of bandages:

- Crepe or elasticised roller bandages are versatile and simple to use.
- Triangular bandages are used for a number of applications, such as supporting an injured arm, completely enveloping a foot or hand, and bandaging the head. In these applications, they are not pressure bandages and will not prevent bleeding. They are used to protect injuries such as burns and grazes where bleeding is not the major concern.
- Ring bandages are used for penetration wounds (see page 18) where a foreign object is protruding from the wound, or in the case of a fracture, when the end of the bone is protruding.

When applying a bandage, follow this procedure:

1. Stand in front of the victim (who should, preferably, be seated or lying down – the latter position being best if the victim is in shock) on his injured side, and place the limb in the position in which it will be bandaged. For instance, a leg or arm is most comfortable when slightly flexed – not dead straight. So don't bandage it that way, unless you think shifting it to what you think is a more comfortable position could make the problem worse – if the end of a broken bone is showing through the skin, for example.
2. Applying an even tension, and rolling the bandage around the limb, bandage the limb to about three bandage widths above and below the wound. If it is a pressure bandage to slow bleeding, finish off with a reef knot, tied directly over the wound. In other cases, if tying a knot, make sure it is not near the injury.
3. If the victim is conscious, confirm that his toes or fingers are not tingling, and that he still has feeling in the extremities. If not, if the extremities are cold to the touch and/or turn blue, the bandage is too tight and should be reapplied with less tension.

A fall from a ladder can result in injuries to limbs, body and head. Make sure that you use the appropriate bandage in all cases.

ASPHYXIATION AND CHOKING

For some obscure reason we all, even adults, tend to shove all sorts of things into our mouths that we shouldn't. So don't! However, accidents do occur; we put washers, nails, screws and assorted items into our mouths when we run out of hands – and we run the risk of asphyxiation. It can be deadly if you don't know what to do.

1. If the victim is conscious, use a finger to remove the blockage from her mouth. If you cannot, bend the victim over, getting her head to about waist height (below the level of the lungs) and thump her hard between her shoulder blades with the heel of your hand. Check to see if the obstruction is visible and can be reached. If so, use two fingers to remove it.

2. If the obstruction has not been forced out, and only then, use the abdominal thrust to expel it. Stand or kneel behind the victim, make a fist with one hand and place it, with the thumb facing inwards, midway between the navel and base of the sternum (breastbone). Now grip your fist with your other hand and pull towards yourself with a quick upward thrust that will force air out of the victim's lungs. Repeat this manoeuvre up to four times, and don't worry about bruising the victim – each thrust must be hard enough to force the obstruction out of the victim's throat.

3. If the victim is unconscious, turn her onto her back and turn her head to one side (this opens the airway). Prise her mouth open and remove the item causing the problem. Do this by putting your first and second fingers into the victim's mouth and pulling the obstruction out of the air passage. If you cannot remove the item blocking the airway, kneel astride the victim and place the heel of one hand in the middle of the chest, midway between the navel and base of the sternum (breastbone). Place your other hand on the first and, keeping your fingers clear of the sternum, push downwards and forwards, keeping your arms straight. (In other words, this is the equivalent of the abdominal thrust described above.) Repeat up to four times, each time with sufficient force to expel the obstruction.

    If this is unsuccessful, begin CPR (see page 22) immediately and call for medical attention, if you have not already done so.

A sharp, upward pull should dislodge the obstruction.

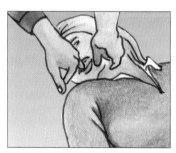

With an unconscious victim, turn the head to one side and remove the obstruction with your fingers.

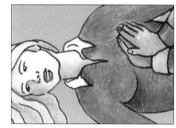

As a last resort, a series of sharp, upward pushes using your body weight should clear the obstruction.

1

2

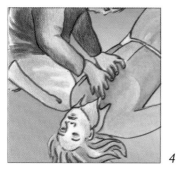

3

4

5

CPR (CARDIOPULMONARY RESUSCITATION)

When a person ceases to breathe her life literally hangs in the balance – she can die within a few minutes.

The reason for the condition might be a blockage of the airway, or the result of an electric shock, to name but two possible causes. The prime concern is to get the victim breathing again and, if her heart has ceased beating, to get that restarted as well.

1. With the victim flat on her back, turn her head to one side, open her mouth and clear away any vomit or blockage using two fingers. Then move her head back to face the ceiling and, placing one hand on her forehead to hold the back of her head against the floor, place your other hand under her neck to tilt it back to open the airway.
2. Pinch her nostrils between the forefinger and thumb of one hand, and pull her mouth open by placing your thumb on her chin and pulling down. Ensure the head is still tilted back.
3. Open your mouth, take a deep breath, seal your lips around the victim's open mouth and deliver a quick, full breath. Repeat this four times as quickly as possible, ensuring each time that the victim's chest rises to maximum expansion. If the chest does not rise and fall as expected, ensure you have her head in the correct position; if there is still no reaction, assume there is an obstruction and treat for choking or asphyxiation (see page 21).
4. If the victim's heart has ceased beating, you will have to use chest compression. Position your hands correctly by first locating the middle of the sternum, and the point where the sternum meets the bottom pair of ribs. The area between the two is the pressure point where you should place the heel of your hand.
5. Raise the fingers of your hand so that the heel of the hand is the only point of contact, and splay them. Now place your other hand on the first, placing the fingers between the splayed fingers of the first hand, and, keeping your arms straight, press down sharply about 40 mm.
6. Allow the chest to return to its original position and repeat the manoeuvre 15 times, at the rate of 80 per minute (roughly three times every two seconds). Follow this with mouth-to-mouth ventilation, and then repeat the sequence of chest depressions. This sequence should be repeated four times per minute until medical assistance arrives or the victim's heart starts beating on its own, at which stage you should cease the compressions immediately. Place the victim in the recovery position as illustrated (see page 23).

HEART ATTACK!

Heart attacks are potentially life-threatening and if anyone tells you he has a severe chest pain, which has spread to one or both arms, neck and jaw, suspect a heart attack. The victim might also feel faint, giddy, be breathless and sweat a great deal. The pain comes on suddenly.

- Lie the victim down in a half-sitting position, head and shoulders supported with pillows or cushions, and the knees bent.
- Loosen clothing around the neck, chest and waist, reassure him and keep him still, and summon medical help immediately.
- Should the victim pass out, place him in the recovery position (see page 22).

Place the victim in a semi-sitting position if he is conscious, or in the recovery position if he is unconscious.

ELECTRIC SHOCK

Electric shock can range from relatively mild, for instance from a faulty telephone line, to a deadly shock from the back of a TV set which, even though it has been switched off, can still be dangerous. Its severity depends on a range of factors such as the current's strength and the amount of time the victim was exposed to it, the amount of insulation protecting the victim (if he was standing on a wet surface the shock will be greater) and the victim's state of health. For instance, if the victim has a weak heart, he could die from a shock that another person would survive.

- If the victim has gripped the appliance shocking him, switch off the power to it or, if you cannot reach the switch, use a dry wooden broomstick or beam to release the grip.
- Smother any clothing that is burning or smouldering, and check that the victim's heart is beating and that he is breathing. If either is absent, call for medical assistance and, in the meantime, administer artificial ventilation and/or chest compression treatment as appropriate (see page 22).
- Once the heartbeat and breathing have resumed, place the victim in the recovery position.

6

HINT

Milk will help alleviate the pain of poison or plant sap in the eye. It might even be a sight-saver!

MIND THOSE EYES

Foreign objects in the eye are probably the most common problem we face, and fortunately in most cases they are little more than an irritant.

The other common problem is that of chemicals, liquids or fumes affecting the eyes.

- If an object is in the eye, stop the victim rubbing it – he will want to, but it will only make the problem worse.
- Tilt the victim's head back and gently pull the eyelid back. If you can see the object, try to wash it out with sterile eyewash in an eye irrigator. If that doesn't work, gently pour lukewarm tap water from a jug over the eye. If you still have no success, carefully remove it with the corner of a damp clean cloth, or a wet cotton bud.
- If you cannot see the object, or cannot remove it (if it is embedded in the eye, **do not** attempt to remove it), cover the eye with an eye pad and seek medical attention.
- In the case of a chemical or liquid in the eye, irrigate it to wash the substance out of the eye. Even if the victim is comfortable afterwards, it is as well to have the eye examined to ensure no permanent damage has been done.
- The bottom line is: wear safety glasses or, when working in the kitchen, keep your head inclined away from frying fat and/or cover the frying food with a purpose-made cover. Hot fat in the eye can ruin your dinner!

GAS AND FUME INHALATION

- When using anything that gives off fumes the golden rule is: always work in a well-ventilated space or out in the open air, if possible. This includes working on your car – if the weather is bad and you're working on the engine, open the garage door, other-wise you could end up with carbon monoxide poisoning, and dead, if you run the engine for any length of time.
- You should also wear a face mask with the appropriate filter. Bear in mind that cleaning fluids, fires, leaks, electrical shorts and a host of other causes can produce harmful fumes or gases.
- If a person has inhaled fumes, the first thing to do is to remove him from the source. Get him out into the open air and lie him down with his head lower than the rest of his body. If he has stopped breathing, commence artificial ventilation immediately and call for medical assistance.

POISONED?

A poison is a substance that, when taken into the body in sufficient quantity, affects the workings of the body and its organs either temporarily or more permanently, possibly damaging parts of the body or causing death in the worst case. Many cases of accidental poisoning occur when children drink dangerous substances stored in cool-drink bottles.

- If the victim is conscious, try to find out what he drank.
- If he is unconscious, check for any possible cause of the problem. Symptoms of poisoning include stomach pain, delirium, convulsions, retching or vomiting, burns around the mouth, throat and gullet and pain in these areas. The victim might also suffer from diarrhoea, have difficulty breathing and lose consciousness.
- If he has swallowed a substance that burns, such as bleach, give him about 500 ml of milk or water to dilute the poison in the stomach.
- If he is unconscious, place him in the recovery position (see page 22) and call for medical attention.

Poisoning can also occur from spider bites, snakebite and poisonous plants (see page 137). Symptoms of poisoning from these causes often include the following: vomiting, nausea, difficulty in breathing, headache, shock, sharp pain and swelling around the site of a bite, one or two puncture wounds, blurred vision.

- Wherever possible, try to identify the species that caused the problem and seek medical attention immediately.
- If breathing stops, begin artificial ventilation immediately.
- If the victim is conscious, carry him to a vehicle and get him to medical attention. Keep him calm and his movements as few as possible, because anything that causes the heart to beat harder will distribute the poison around his body quicker – and the aim is to keep it as localised as possible.

SNAKEBITE!
The first sign of a bite is usually a sharp pain and swelling around the site of the bite – usually two small puncture wounds. (It could be only one puncture, however, if the snake managed to get only one fang to penetrate the skin.) So do not assume one mark can only be a sting. The victim might start having difficulty seeing properly, he may feel nauseous, may vomit, and have difficulty breathing.

- Keep the victim still and calm, and reassure him – the vast majority of victims survive being bitten by a snake, but fear can bring on shock.
- The site of the bite should be kept below the level of the heart, so if the person has been bitten on the ankle, sit him against a wall or tree or, if you're on a slope, lie him down with his feet down-slope.
- Wipe any venom away from the bite site, apply a dry, sterile dressing to the wound and encourage the victim to keep still.
- If the snake is still around, try to identify it, and summon medical attention if it is a poisonous species (there are excellent books available that will help you identify the various species).
- If the victim stops breathing, begin mouth-to-mouth ventilation immediately.
- Do not tie a tourniquet around the limb above the bite and do not try to suck the poison out of the bite or cut it in an effort to make it bleed.

People generally survive snakebites. Keep the victim calm and keep the bite area below the level of the heart.

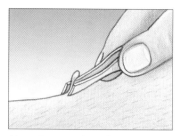

Use sharp-pointed tweezers, gripping the sting below the poison sac, to remove the sting.

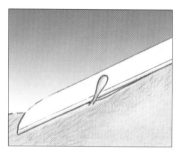

No tweezers? Use a knife blade, laid at an angle of about 30 degrees against the skin, to scrape the sting out.

- Keep the patient calm and carry him to a car to get him to hospital, if that is the course of action you have to take. The less he moves, the lower his heart rate will be.
- A final thought: try not to kill the snake! Despite what you might be thinking at the time, they do a lot of good. Have someone keep an eye on it, and contact your local snake-catcher, if there is one, to have it removed.

BEE STING? BE GONE!

Bee stings are quite common and not life-threatening unless the victim is allergic to this sort of sting. Where much of the pain results, however, is when another person, trying to help, uses tweezers to grab the sac at the end of the sting and pull it out. It does usually work – the sting comes out, but as the sac has been squeezed in the process, the poison in it has been pushed into the victim.

So, if you do not have fine-pointed tweezers that will enable you to grip the sting **below** the sac, simply use a knife blade to scrape the sting out of the skin. Hold the blade at a flat angle to the skin, and sweep the sting out.

Signs of the sting should vanish soon thereafter. Use a cold compress to speed relief, but if symptoms continue for more than a few hours, consult your doctor.

SPLINTERS . . . SMALL BUT PAINFUL

Anyone who says the small things don't count hasn't had a splinter embedded in their skin.

If this occurs, wash the area. Then use tweezers that have been sterilised in a flame to remove it. If the splinter is too deep, however, do not probe the skin for it – it could cause an infection. Rather go to your doctor to have it removed.

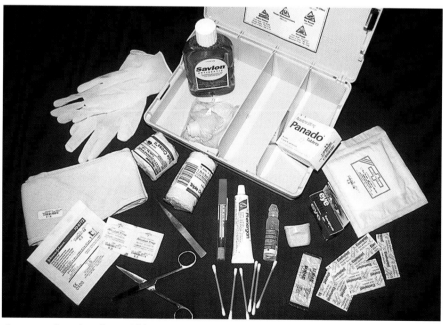

A comprehensive first-aid kit is essential in the home.

THE ESSENTIAL FIRST-AID KIT

Every home should have a first-aid kit in a childproof, purpose-made box available from a pharmacy, and it should be kept out of the reach of children.

These kits are essentially for minor injuries and ailments around the home – from cuts and sprains to headaches. However, it should also have what is required to treat more serious injuries while the victim is awaiting medical assistance.

The basic kit should comprise the following:

- Antiseptic solution for use with cotton wool when cleaning wounds
- Antiseptic wipes for the same purpose
- Two or three elasticised bandages
- A range of plasters of different sizes and shapes
- At least one roll of fabric-backed plaster plus a pair of blunt-nosed scissors
- Tweezers
- Cotton buds (ear buds)
- Two or three triangular bandages plus the same number of safety pins
- Sterile dressings
- Antihistamine cream to treat insect bites and stings
- Eye drops
- Sterile eye dressings
- Sterile eyewash
- Eyebath
- Aspirin or paracetamol tablets
- A pack of surgical gloves
- Mouth-to-mouth device
- Tubular bandage and application tongs for the treatment of wounds to fingers
- Thermometer and/or heat-sensitive strip

Points to remember

- Where possible, use pills sealed in foil for longer life.
- Stick a sheet of paper into the inside of the kit's lid, with all the important emergency numbers for your area.
- Make a habit of checking expiry dates of all the medicines in the home, plus those in the first-aid kit, and discard those that have expired. Flush them down the toilet.

HINT

This is not really first aid – but it is good sense. Some medications may have unwelcome side-effects in some individuals. So, if your doctor prescribes a course of medication and you are unsure whether it will agree with you or not, get only a portion of the prescription at first. If it works without any unpleasant side-effects, you can always get the rest of the course. If not, ask your doctor to prescribe an alternative. Since medicines cannot be returned, you might have wasted some money, but not as much as should you have purchased the full course.

Secondly, always complete the full course of the treatment – and don't stop when the symptoms disappear, as your system needs those last few doses of the medicine to defeat the ailment completely.

general

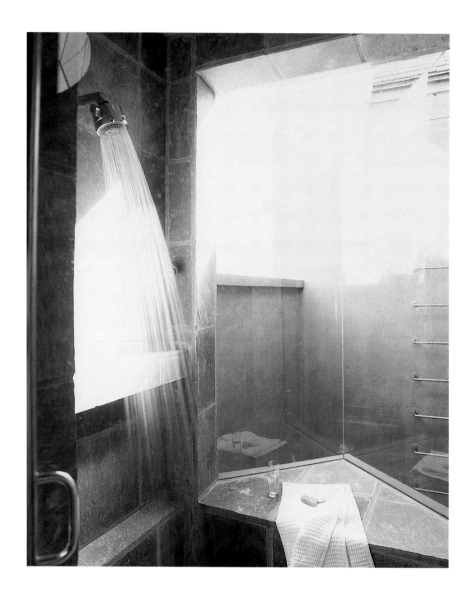

Being able to make small repairs around the home and to your vehicle, and to find inventive uses for everything from toothpicks to lengths of wire, can save you a great deal of money and give you a sense of accomplishment. So let's take a look at some cost- and time-saving things you can do around the home. But before we do, remember this: if you don't know how to . . . don't! This is particularly true when dealing with anything electrical (since a mistake can cost a life) and plumbing, where a mistake can cause major damage.

CAUTION
You should not make any changes, additions or repairs to the fixed wiring of your home. If you need to have any of this work done, you should contact a registered electrician to do it for you.

Previous page: *Tiling around an awkward shape? Use a few tile tricks (see p. 60).* This page: *Shower and bath outlets can become blocked. Careful use of caustic soda (see p. 56) will help you have a trouble-free shower again!*

ELECTRICAL

FIND THAT FAULT!

When an appliance develops a fault the remedy is sometimes quite simple, so start with the basics:

1. Unplug the appliance, plug a bedside light or other appliance into the wall socket and check that the power is coming through – you could be wasting you time working on the appliance.
2. Assuming the power supply is fine, check the basics of the appliance – Are the plug connections sound? Is the flex in good repair? If both are OK, check the connections between the flex and the appliance. If the appliance has a fuse in the circuit, check to see if that is also sound.
3. If all these aspects are OK, then the fault is somewhere else. Look for burned areas surrounding any component. If you smell an 'electric' smell as well, that merely reinforces the evidence.
4. If the damaged component is one you can replace simply, then do so, but if not, take the appliance in for repair.

FIX THAT FAULT!

If you feel capable of doing the repair yourself, follow this procedure:

1. Clearly identify the make, model and year of manufacture of the appliance and the name, code and other details of the component, and purchase the exact equivalent. Do not remove the faulty component yet.
2. Once you have the replacement part, place it in the same relative position as the faulty one and make sure it is compatible. Then remove any connections one at a time, labelling each one as you go – A, B, C, or use a simple bar code. Simultaneously, mark the connection points on the faulty item.
3. Now connect the replacement – because you have marked each wire and the replacement is the twin of the faulty one, you should have no trouble connecting it up correctly.
4. Do a double check of your connections, plug in and switch on – but only for a second. If you don't smell any 'electric' smell, your repair is probably fine and you can use the appliance normally.

WOODY WOOD PLUCKER

Dry wood is an effective insulator – and we emphasise **dry** wood. So, if you need to work on anything electrical, and the floor is damp, lay a couple of lengths of timber on the floor, with a stout plank on top. Stand on the plank, so that you are clear of any moisture.

Secondly, if a victim of electric shock has grasped the appliance, for instance, and cannot let go, and you cannot get to the power supply in a hurry to turn it off, use a wooden beam (such as a broomstick) to force them off it. And don't be gentle – severe bruising or a broken arm is preferable to the alternative.

CAUTION

■ **Never** replace a blown fuse with one of a higher rating; instead of blowing a fuse, you'll probably damage a component.
■ Even when you think you have found the fault, keep on checking – damage to one component could have caused damage to a second.
■ The first time you touch the appliance after working on it, remember to do so with the back of your hand; if there is a short you will get a momentary shock, but your hand will not grip anything.

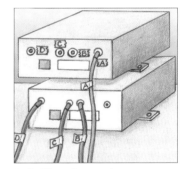

Labelling the cords as you change them makes it easier to ensure you make the right connections.

USE IT SAFELY

Water and electricity go together in a relatively limited range of applications, such as kettles, geysers, and so on. In other applications, for example toasters, putting the two together is dangerous.

- Don't use an appliance if the floor is damp.
- Don't use a toaster, for example, if water has been spilt on it; even though you might have dried the outside very well, the workings could still be soaking – and deadly.
- Switch off and unplug the appliance, rest it in a position in which any water can drip out, and leave it in the hot sun for a few hours to dry completely.
- When trying a toaster again, place a couple of slices of bread in position, depress the lever and only then plug in the unit and switch on the power. If there is still moisture present, it will probably trip your earth leakage relay.

MAKING THE RIGHT CONNECTIONS

Connecting a plug is simple, but get it wrong and you – or someone else – could have a much shorter life.

1. Remove the outer sheath of the cord to a length of about 25 mm, exposing the three inner flexes. When doing this, ensure that you do not damage the insulation of the latter. Then strip the last 6-8 mm of insulation off each inner flex. You're now ready to make the connection.
2. When connecting a three-core cable, the brown insulated wire goes to the live pin – marked with an L on the plastic of the plug – and the blue insulated wire (the neutral wire) goes to the small pin with the N impressed into the plastic of the plug.
3. The wire with green-and-yellow-striped insulation is your earth wire and this goes **only** to the large pin at the top of the plug, furthest from the point at which the cord meets the plug. **Never** connect this wire to either of the small pins.
4. Ensure that the cord's outer insulation is gripped by the two flaps of the plug, or by the saddle clamp that is used in some types.

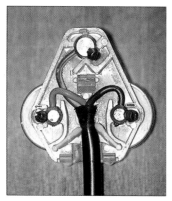

Connecting a plug correctly isn't difficult. Just ensure that the grips hold the outer insulation as well.

HONEY, MAY I BORROW YOUR HAIR DRYER?

Who says a hair dryer is just for drying hair? A word of warning though: make sure you have your partner's permission to use her dryer for these tasks, or the subject is sure to come up at dinner (if she makes you any!).

- Need to get that braai fire going properly? A hair dryer will do the job in seconds – just make sure you hold it well away from the fire so that the heat doesn't melt the dryer's plastic.
- Is your store of odds and ends full of dust, sawdust and shavings? Use a gentle breeze from a hair dryer to get rid of the debris without all the hassle of picking the bits out.

CONNECTING ELECTRICAL CORDS – NOW HERE'S A STAGGERING THOUGHT!

When you're connecting two- or three-core cords together, staggering the connections will ensure that your connection is safer. Just ensure that you connect earth to earth, live to live and neutral to neutral.

NOTE: Join cords only as a last resort. Any join compromises the integrity of the cord, for example by providing a means for moisture to penetrate.

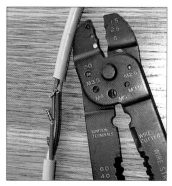

A safer, neater connection.

REPLACE THAT SWITCH

Bear in mind that though light switches and wall sockets are freely available from hardware shops, as mentioned elsewhere, by law only a qualified and registered electrician is allowed to work on the fixed wiring in a home. And working on wall sockets and light switches constitutes working on the fixed wiring. So, unless you are absolutely certain of your abilities, leave this alone – and get an electrician to do it.

But, assuming you're like the writer (who knows what he's doing), this is how to change a wall switch:

1. Safety first – ensure that the mains power is turned off, the family is aware of what you're doing, and you have pasted a big notice next to the mains switch telling everyone to **LEAVE IT ALONE!** Turn off **all** the switches on the main circuit board. Switch the TV or stereo or a mains-powered radio on and crank up the volume – so that should anyone ignore the notice, or forget you're working and turn on the power, you might be deafened, but you'll get some warning at least.
2. Remove the cover plate and the two securing screws for the faulty switch. For extra safety, mark each wire's position. Note that the fixed wiring in the suburban home has a different colour coding to that used on appliances: **red** is **live**, **black** is **neutral** and **green** is **earth**.
3. Connect each wire in turn, double-checking at each stage.
4. Once you are completely satisfied that your connections are sound and correct, replace the switch in the wall, using the securing screws to fix it in position.
5. Now (first turning off whatever you set up as your DIY alarm) go to the main distribution board, turn the mains switch back on and, one switch at a time, turn on each circuit. If the earth leakage trips at any stage, there's a chance you made a mistake when connecting up the new switch. If all is fine, however, switch off everything again, and replace the cover plate on your new switch and plug in a bedside light.
6. Switch everything back on again, and switch the light on. If you see the light, you have succeeded. Well done.

Remove the cover and holding screws and gently pull the switch assembly out of its recess.

Working in sequence, disconnect the wire from the faulty switch and attach it to the corresponding terminal on the replacement.

Note that the earth connection on the replacement is attached to the base plate. Make a final check to confirm that the new connections are correct, replace the switch and test.

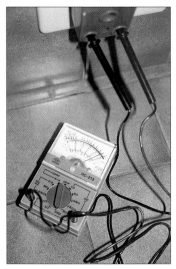

A multipurpose multimeter makes testing circuits simple – but follow the tips on the right.

Want a useful instrument around the home? A multitester is a good choice.

They're also known as volt-ohm meters and are extremely useful when you're checking an electrical circuit. Their selector allows them to be used to measure direct and alternating voltages, direct current, and resistance decibels.

- Each usually has a range of operating values, say 10, 50, 250 and 500 volts DC. Always set the instrument to the range you intend testing – for example, if checking the mains AC voltage, don't set the instrument to 10 or 50 volts, but to 250 or 500.
- When you are unsure of the voltage or current, always set the instrument to the highest value and test. Then reduce it if necessary and test again, until you obtain a reading you can read off.
- Always ensure that you zero the instrument every time you use it or change the function or setting.

THE COST OF DOING YOUR OWN ELECTRICAL WORK

In many cases you will save money doing your own work, but bear in mind that the SABS code of practice requires all fixed wiring in a home to be carried out either by or under the supervision of a registered and qualified electrician.

So, let's say you make changes to your electrical system – be it adding a ceiling fan or security light – and at some stage decide to sell your home. Well, if your work is not up to standard or you have used materials that do not conform to the required specifications, you will be obliged to have the work redone before your home gets a clean bill of health.

CAR CARE

AVOID THE GARAGE CRUNCH

There's little worse than parking your car in your garage, or finding it parked in the garage so far over that you cannot get in. However, there is an easy way to have everyone align the car perfectly every time: park it exactly where you want it, then tie a marker to a piece of string so that it touches the windscreen directly in front of the driver's eyes and directly above the steering wheel. All the driver has to do is drive into the garage (straight, of course), and ease on until the marker touches the windscreen in the abovementioned position.

Even the worst driver should be able to get this one right!

Align your car every time in the garage, and avoid a lot of frustration.

Ample storage space is crucial to a comfortable home – especially in the bedroom. A few simple changes (see p. 39)
will help you make the most of your cupboards.

Goodbye, Mr Chips – this idea isn't just a pipe dream.

A cable tie, a spare key, and you'll be free of the hassle of calling the locksmith when you lock your keys in the car.

This is a last resort, but should keep you going until you can get a new radiator.

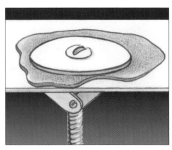

Fried eggs anyone? A simple repair like this is, again, only an emergency quick-fix – replace the radiator as soon as you can.

GIVE THAT PIPE A SECOND LIFE . . .

Swimming pool hoses have to be replaced every so often, but don't discard all of the sections. Select one and slip it over a wooden dowel (an old broomstick will do fine) and tie it up against your garage or carport wall at a height at which it will stop your car door hitting the wall – a simple solution to nasty chips.

OH NO! LOCKED THE KEYS IN AGAIN!

Little is as upsetting as slamming your car door – and seeing your ignition keys dangling invitingly from the ignition. Calling in a locksmith can cost you a bit, quite apart from the frustration and delays this sort of thing causes.

So, pick a spot on the underside of the car which is not visible and where a spare key can rest and attach it firmly, using two or three cable ties, if you wish.

Next time you lock your keys in the car, dive underneath, cut the spare free – and smile!

Don't forget to put the key back – but in a different spot; if anyone saw you perform the trick, they might, if they're that way inclined, decide to use the key to borrow your car. If your car has hubcaps, putting the key in one is a good idea. Use some Prestik to hold it in place – as close to the centre as possible.

RADIATOR RUNNING REPAIRS

These repairs are very temporary – just to give you time to get your car to the garage. They are not intended to save you the cost of having the job done properly.

- If a tube in your radiator develops a leak, carefully cut it at the point of corrosion, bend each end back and close it off with a pair of pliers. Coolant loss should be slowed enough for you to make it to the workshop.
- If the body develops a leak, put a large washer and rubber gasket onto a hollow-wall toggle bolt of sufficient length to fit into the body, first dry-fitting the washer and gasket and bending the former to match the curve of the body if necessary. Now enlarge the leak hole just enough to admit the closed wings of the toggle bolt and tighten.

DON'T PULL UP IN A CLOUD OF RUST

Cars, particularly if you live on the coast, are in constant danger of rust. Here are a few tips to keep rust at bay for as long as possible:

- If you buy a car new, spend a bit extra and have an electronic rust preventer installed.
- Check the drain holes at the base of the doors; if they have rubber seals on them, consider removing them. The seals are intended to allow water to drain out, but prevent dust coming in. Sometimes, however, they help clog the drain holes and slow the escape of water, so increasing the possibility of rust.

- Have the vehicle rustproofed upon purchase, and at regular intervals thereafter (check with the AA or a reputable company doing this sort of work).
- Keep your car under cover if not in a garage, to prevent dew forming on it.
- If you live near the coast or are holidaying there, washing the car regularly with ordinary tap water will help rid it of harmful salt deposits and prevent the onset of rust.
- Treat even the smallest paint chip or scratch as soon as possible – preventing rust is better than trying to cure it.

RUST: REMOVE IT, AND REPAIR IT

1. Begin by removing the rust deposit with sandpaper or a small wire wheel mounted on an electric drill or angle grinder. Remove as little paint around the rusted area as possible, but ensure that all loose rust is entirely removed.
2. Now apply a coat of rust converter. This seals the remaining rust, on which you can apply primer and then your final coats of paint. Once the paint has cured, rub it down using progressively finer sandpaper until you achieve the desired result.

NOTE: This sort of repair is aimed at derusting and making good small chips and scratches on cars and trailers, for example. For larger repairs, it is better to have the work done professionally.

A TOUCHING SOLUTION . . .

When using spray paint to touch up those little chips and scratches in your car's paintwork, you can avoid spraying areas you don't wish to, and the sharp edges that result from using masking tape, like this:

Cut a small hole in a piece of paper. The shape of the hole should roughly follow the shape of the damaged area, and be only slightly larger than the area. Hold the piece of paper 25 mm away from the bodywork, and the spray nozzle at the required distance. The spray stream will be confined to the area of damage, but the edge will be soft and you will achieve a much better result.

Remove the loose rust, confining your work to as small an area as possible.

Apply a coat of rust converter.

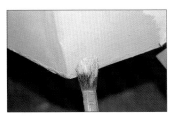

Apply the primer.

Spray the repaired area and finish by rubbing down the area to match the surrounds.

Holding the card a couple of centimetres from the side of the vehicle will avoid sharp edges to your touch-up job.

A small metal plate slipped under the jack when changing a wheel in soft sand will prevent its sinking into the soft surface.

Use a pipe to increase the leverage.

Need to get oil to a spot you cannot reach with the can? Just use a piece of wire – you can even bend the wire to avoid obstructions.

TOOL TRICKS

The essential tool kit for your car (plus an item or two you might not have thought of) is just part of the story. For, although a tool should be used only for its designed purpose, there are times when a couple of tools or other aids can be used in conjunction to tackle a task.

You're out on the road, the car starts to falter and then fails. This is not the time to discover that the very tool you should have in your tool box is the one you don't have, so, first of all, take a look at our selection. It may look pretty extensive, but there are some items that could make all the difference in an emergency, even though you will seldom use them otherwise.

- Tool box
- Torch, preferably with emergency flasher
- Plastic putty
- Exhaust bandage and compound
- Coil of thin wire
- Selection of cable ties
- Tie-down straps
- Mini-hacksaw
- Clean cloth
- Hand cleaner
- Roll of duct tape
- Syphon for transferring fuel
- Warning triangle
- Tyre inflator – aerosol or electric
- Socket set – small
- Vice grip
- Adjustable spanner – small and medium
- Long-nose pliers
- Sidecutter
- Screwdriver set
- Tyre gauge
- Valve spanner
- Selection of fuses
- Plug socket spanner
- Tow rope
- Jumper leads
- Fire extinguisher

MAKE YOUR OWN WET-AND-DRY VACUUM ATTACHMENT

Using the household vacuum, whether a wet-and-dry type or not, to mop up a mess in the garage might seriously endanger your marriage, so make your own wet-and-dry attachment. You will need a bucket that can be sealed (a large container for dry granular pool chlorine is ideal), a length of vacuum pipe, two lengths of PVC piping which will fit the vacuum pipe, and the pipe to your garage vacuum, or household vacuum.

1. Make two holes for the PVC pipes in the bucket's lid. Glue the one PVC pipe into the lid so that it protrudes about 50 mm above the lid and to about 100 mm above the bottom of the container. This pipe is the inlet.
2. The second length of PVC pipe can be much shorter, and should protrude into the container as little as possible – 10 mm or so – with the other 50 mm being above the lid.
3. Place the lid on the container and connect the vacuum to the short PVC pipe. Connect your other length of vacuum pipe to the second pipe, and you're ready to go.
4. Switch on, and the vacuum draws debris into the container for later disposal.

This attachment is also great for picking up small items that you have spilled – like panel pins and small screws – for later retrieval. And you don't endanger your marriage.

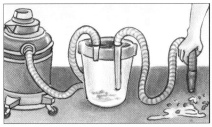

This simple wet-and-dry attachment enables you to use your ordinary household vacuum to mop up spills – without the subject coming up at dinner!

STORAGE

MULTIPLY THOSE SHELVES

Bottles, jars and cans come in a variety of sizes and heights – which leaves most of the area between shelves unoccupied. Make up loose shelves that fit into the cupboard. They are self-supporting, you can adapt them any time you like, and you will make much better use of the cupboard. Ensure the fit is snug so that the shelves cannot slip off their supports.

MAKE THE MOST OF YOUR WARDROBE

Most built-in cupboards are tall enough to accommodate two hanger rails, so why not add a second for the wardrobe in which you keep suits, jackets and slacks? Ladies' wardrobes can get the same treatment, but if the wardrobe also contains long garments such as evening dresses, suspend the second hanger rail on cord and make it long enough, but allow space at one end for the longer garments to hang freely. Raise the top rail a little if necessary.

This handy shelf within a shelf lets you make more use of the storage space.

This unit, made from 6-mm plywood and drawer runners, is sized to fit snugly into the shelf width. A spacer on the door side ensures that the trays can pass the door.

THIS SHOE IS A GOOD IDEA

It's difficult keeping shoes tidy, isn't it? No, it's not. A simple unit like this, comprising sliding trays instead of shelves and fitting snugly so that the runners operate as normal, works wonders.

PIPE DREAMS

Storing items such as garden tools, lengths of timber and so on can be difficult – but try this: fill a sturdy box with PVC pipe offcuts or cardboard tubes used to mail large documents. Now you'll be able to store the abovementioned items neatly, without their falling over.

LIQUID SOLUTIONS. CHEERS!

Here are a few tips that just go to show that some things do go better . . . with a particular brand of cool drink.

Stained toilet?
Pour a can of the cool drink into the toilet bowl. Let it sit for about an hour, then flush. The acid in the drink removes stains from vitreous china.

Rusty bumper?
To remove rust spots from chrome fittings on your car, try rubbing them with a crumpled-up piece of aluminium foil dipped in the cool drink.

Corrosion on car battery terminals?
Pour the product over the terminals to bubble away the corrosion.

Loosen a rusted bolt?
Try putting a cloth soaked in the cool drink on the rusted bolt for several minutes.
   If the nut is on a horizontal surface, you can also use child's plasticine to build a dam around it, pour a little drink into the reservoir you have created, and leave it to stand for a while.

Want to bake a moist ham?
Empty a can of the cool drink into the baking pan, wrap the ham in aluminium foil, and bake. Thirty minutes before the ham is finished, remove the foil, allowing the drippings to mix with the cool drink for sumptuous brown gravy.

Get grease off clothes?
Simply empty a can of the cool drink into a load of greasy clothes, add detergent, and run through a regular cycle.

Clean your car's windscreen?
The cool drink will help loosen grease stains and you can also use it to clean road haze from your windshield.

And you thought it was only for drinking!
   For those who like detail, the cool drink's active ingredient is phosphoric acid and its pH is 2,8.

ADHESIVES AND GLUES

A TAPE IN TIME . . .
Lay masking tape along each edge of the surfaces you are going to glue together, apply the glue and allow the excess to ooze out. Remove it, and then remove the strips of tape – the surfaces abutting the join will be clean and glue-free.

Apply tape along the edge of the join.

SUPPORT THAT PLATE
Repairing a favourite plate that has been broken will not return it to its previous glory but, with luck, you'll get reasonably close.

   The key is to support the plate in an attitude that won't cause the pieces to fall to one side – and the way to do that is by embedding the largest section of the plate vertically in a bucket of sand before glueing the pieces together. It makes the job a great deal easier.

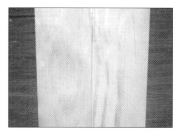

Excess glue is removed when the tape is removed.

IT'S OK, MY CHINA
Avoid the problem of glue marring your repair:

1. Taking great care to avoid getting any onto the broken surface, apply a light coating of petroleum jelly to the area along the break – use the tip of your finger and sweep it lightly **towards** the break line.
2. Do the same to the piece to be glued into position.
3. Apply the glue as directed, and press the two surfaces together – excess glue will squeeze out but will be unable to take hold on the outer surface and can be removed later.

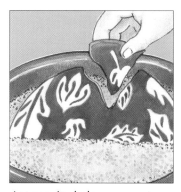

Let gravity help you – put the plate in a position in which the pieces won't fall to one side.

NEED TO KNOW WHEN THE GLUE HAS CURED?
Use a little extra and glue two pieces of the same material together, then try to separate them some time later. If you can, then you know the workpiece also probably still has a little time to go.

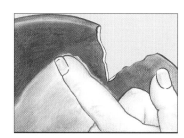

The lightest coating stops glue marring the surface.

CLEVER USES FOR SYRINGES
Syringes make cheap and effective dispensers in a variety of applications and are available from pharmacies. When buying one, consider getting a thick needle at the same time – and file down the tip so that it is too blunt to penetrate skin. Then . . .

- Use it as a handy glue gun to deliver precise amounts of glue, in the tiniest quantities, right where you want it. It's probably best to confine this use to water-based glues for use on wood and paper, for instance. If the needle you have used is large enough, a straight pin can be used to seal it when not in use.
- Use it as a grease gun.
- Use it as an oil gun.
- The ardent cake-maker can use a syringe to make some really intricate designs when applying icing.

A hacksaw blade or bowsaw blade, as illustrated, scores the surface so that the glue sticks better.

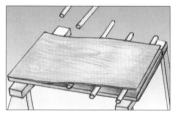

Align the end precisely, then withdraw the dowels or battens one by one and press the laminate into position.

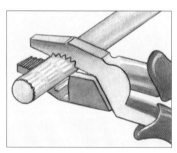

Groovy – and at a fraction of the cost of the purchased item.

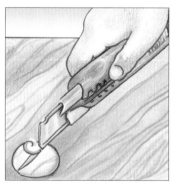

Your veneer getting a lift? Use a glue-filled straw to get the glue to exactly where you need it.

HERE'S A WOOLLY IDEA

Tease out a small amount of wire wool and use it to strengthen that join by sprinkling some across the join.

BUT WILL IT STICK?

Why remove old laminate? It's such a chore. Instead, make a scorer out of an old hacksaw blade or a bowsaw blade, as illustrated, screwed tightly between two pieces of 13 mm × 44 mm pine about 300 mm long. Now scrape the blade over the surface of the old laminate, clear away the fragments, apply the glue and lay the new surface. See, much easier.

AND AS FOR GLUEING LAMINATES . . .

It's essential that a laminate be positioned exactly. So, once the contact glue on both surfaces is dry to the touch and the laminate is ready to be applied, place a number of strips of timber across the width of the laminate at intervals of 250 mm or so (dowels work well). Align the laminate exactly and withdraw the timber or dowels one at a time, starting from one end and working down the ranks.

HOW'S THIS FOR A GROOVY TIP?

Lengths of dowel cut to length make good substitutes for purpose-made dowels available from your local hardware store. But you need to ensure that excess glue can escape. Easy!

Having cut the dowel to length, make grooves along its length by gripping it firmly with a pair of pliers. The grooves on the pliers' jaws create channels in the dowel, allowing excess glue to escape.

A NOZZLE IDEA

As a glue bottle approaches empty, you have to wait longer and longer for the dregs to reach the end of the nozzle. So, while you're using the bottle, store it upside down between applications. Then you won't have any delay as you apply the glue. Just make sure you replace the cap properly every time!

A SOLUTION ON THE LIGHTER SIDE

Trying to remove a mirror that has been fixed in position with mirror tape? Get some lighter fluid onto the pieces of tape, and you'll be able to prise the mirror off after two or three minutes. No scratches, no marks – and the remnants of tape can be removed easily.

BLOWING . . . BUBBLES – THE LAST STRAW

- Edge of the veneer lifting? Suck a little glue into a straw (or a syringe) and force it under the area that has lifted, then apply pressure until the glue has set.
- And when a blister develops, carefully remove a thin sliver along the grain of the veneer (not across it) and check the fit. Remove a little more material if necessary. Then, using the same method as above, get glue under the lifted area, press it down, wipe off excess glue and leave under pressure until the glue has cured.

NAIL THE PROBLEM – AN APPEALING SOLUTION
Laminate lifted, peeling off? Need to use contact adhesive? Easy, just prop up the laminate with nails and apply the glue to both surfaces. When they are dry to the touch, remove the nails, and press the laminate back down in position.

A THREAD IN TIME
Tighten up that chair-leg strut with thread when glue won't do the job. Whip the thread around the strut, apply glue and allow to dry. Then glue the strut in position as normal.

NOT SUCH A DUSTY IDEA
Another idea to tighten up a loose join: mix the glue with sawdust, and use it to secure the join – the wood in the glue will give it extra strength and help pack the join tightly.

A NEW MEANING FOR WEDGWOOD?
Get a really tight fit like this: split the end of the chair strut you're reglueing into its socket, and push a wedge of wood a little way into the split. Now apply glue to the socket and insert the strut. As the strut goes into its socket, the end of the wedge comes up against the bottom of the socket and is forced into the strut, spreading the halves and making for a really tight fit!

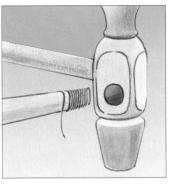

We'll have a quick whip round and then finish the job: thread whipped round a strut will make for a tighter join.

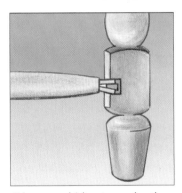

It's a good idea to make the split horizontal so that the pressure is along the axis of the leg. If across it, you could split the leg. Not a good idea.

CLEVER USES FOR TOOTHPICKS
Apart from using them to get rid of those annoying scraps of food trapped between your teeth, toothpicks can be used in a few other ways:

- The obvious use is as a filler for a screw hole in wood.
- But you can also use it to make a temporary repair to a small hole in a hose.
- And when you're cooking sausages, it's sometimes a problem getting them to brown properly. So, just push a toothpick or two through each sausage from side to side so that the ends stick out like the oars on a boat. Now the sausage can't roll back, and you'll be able to brown each side without a hassle.
- Toothpicks make very good mixers for epoxy glues and are good applicators as well.
- Run out of clothes pegs? A toothpick or two threaded through the cloth of a blanket or sheet you wish to dry will keep it on the line where you want it; but don't use this trick on material with a fine weave – use pins in those instances.

HINT
Before using any type of glue – some of which requires the strength of Hercules (or Arnold!) to remove – coat your hands in ordinary dish-washing liquid or soap to prevent it from sticking to your skin.

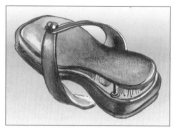

Contact adhesive usually needs time to cure before the surfaces are pressed together. Nails or panel pins are a handy help.

There is a wide range of adhesives to suit just about any purpose.

GOOD FOR THE SOLE

Often a strap comes loose on a shoe that is otherwise perfectly serviceable, so instead of dumping the pair, fix it:

1. Prise the body of the shoe away from the sole and apply contact adhesive to the two surfaces, plus both surfaces of the strap that has come free.
2. Allow time for the glue to cure, according to the maker's instructions – use a nail to keep the two surfaces apart.
3. Position the glued end of the strap on the sole and push the surfaces together. Clamp them tightly for the recommended time, and a pair of shoes has a new lease of life.

A BRIEF GLOSSARY OF ADHESIVES AND GLUES	
Type	**Applications**
White (PVA)	wood, paper, leather, cork, stone
Yellow (carpenter's aliphatic resin)	wood, indoor use
Polyurethane	waterproof – wood, outdoor use
Epoxy	dissimilar materials, nonporous
Urea formaldehyde (powder)	mixed with water, outdoor use on woods – waterproof
Contact	instant bonding, wood, leather, plastics, veneers
Hot glue	melted, applied with glue gun used on wood and other materials
Bolt-locking compound	metal to metal, prevents loosening
Cyanoacrylate	nonporous dissimilar materials, quick-setting
Tile adhesive	ceramic, glazed tiles to plaster

KEYS

THE KEY TO MAKING A MATCH IS . . .
Colour-code your locks and keys so that you can quickly match one with the other. It's irritating when you have to unlock something, and have to go through a number of keys before finding the one that works.

BROKEN KEY STUCK IN THE LOCK?
Try using a jigsaw blade to hook the key out of the slot. Use the blade to raise the tumbler pins so that you can get it in far enough to catch the serration nearest to you, then carefully pull the broken shank out. Do not push the blade in too far, however: you could jam it in the slot, along with the broken shank. If that happens, call a locksmith.

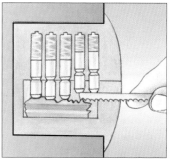

An old jigsaw blade – the narrow one designed for scrolling – will help you get a broken key out of a lock.

Try lubricating a sticky lock with pencil lead (see p. 47).

Mark up accurately and check, then drill the hole for the cylinder.

Install the lock, and trim the cylinder-connecting bar to the required length.

Install the strike plate, using the screws provided to secure it in position.

A great deal safer.

LOCK OUT!

The amount of difficulty you will have installing a new lock depends on the type. Some can simply be attached to the surface of the door and jamb, whereas others require a certain amount of drilling and work to the door and jamb during installation.

A rim night latch, also known as a deadlock night latch, is simple to install and provides good security. This is how to go about installing one:

1. Mark the position of the lock at a convenient height. If the lock kit comes with a paper template, use that; if not, use the lock mounting plate. Bear in mind that you may have to recess the fore-end of the lock's body, so take this into account when marking up. Whether you need to cut recesses for the body fore-end and strike plate will depend on the clearance between the door and the jamb at the point you're installing the lock, though the finished job will probably look neater with the fore-end and strike plate recessed.
2. Having confirmed your marking-up is correct, drill the hole for the cylinder. In our case we used a 30-mm spade bit. Remember to drill through the door until the tip of the bit protrudes on the other side; then complete the hole from that side, otherwise you will chip the wood and not obtain a neat finish.
3. Slip the cylinder into the hole from the front of the door and fix it to the base plate with the two screws provided.
4. Slip the body of the lock onto the connecting bar, check how much clearance there is between the body and the surface of the door, and then remove the excess length of the cylinder connecting bar by the same amount. Confirm that the lock operates properly.
5. Cut the recess, if you are recessing the fore-end, and fix the body of the lock to the base plate.
6. Close the door and mark the position of the strike plate on the doorjamb.
7. Again, cut a recess if necessary, and fix the strike plate in position with the screws provided.

The completed job – simple, and secure.

STICKY LOCK, GET THE LEAD OUT

When you find that a key is difficult to insert into a lock and withdraw, run a lead pencil over some fine sandpaper a few times and cover the key shank with the graphite dust. Now insert the key into the slot a few times. Graphite is a good dry lubricant and the key should soon move freely.

THE KEY TO UNFREEZING A LOCK IS . . .

. . . using the key itself. Warm the shank with a lighter and push it into the lock as normal. It will melt any ice in the barrel and allow it to turn.

WALLS

CHASING A WALL

An angle grinder is an excellent tool for chasing a wall in order to conceal wiring to a new fixture.

1. Mark the path of the channel you are going to chase and use an angle grinder fitted with a masonry disc to complete the task.
2. If the wire you are using has too large a diameter to fit into the channel made by a single cut, make a second one parallel to the first and chip out the plaster between the two. Chase to a depth of about twice the diameter of the wire you're installing – remember, the less you chase, the less you have to fill.
3. Hot-glue the wire at regular intervals to keep it in place.
4. Use interior or exterior filler, as appropriate, to fill the channel, so that the filler's surface is above that of the surrounding wall. Then sand down to a flat finish.

FILLING CRACKS IN WALLS

Hairline cracks can be concealed quite adequately with a coat of paint, but wider fissures will need to be filled.

- Use as little water as possible when mixing the filler so that the mix retains its shape, and apply it with a putty knife.
- If the crack is wide and deep, apply the filler in two or three layers, allowing time between each application to allow the previous layer to dry.
- Fill to a level higher than the surrounding wall, sand down once dry and repaint.
- To stop the filled area appearing too 'flat', roughen it slightly with a wire brush before painting.

Make two parallel grooves if necessary, and carefully chip out the masonry between them. Two would be necessary if you were installing a water pipe, for instance.

If necessary, hot-glue the wire to hold it in position, fill the channel, sand and paint to finish.

CAUTION

If chasing a wall in an area near an existing light switch or power point, check the position of the existing electrical conduit before commencing. Furthermore, the operation is not only very noisy, but produces large amounts of dust, so wear ear protection and a mask and, if working inside, keep the door closed or seal off the area to stop dust permeating the house.

Plastering can also be creative. Here a special effect has been achieved by using a rough texture and a mix of colours.

THE BRICK TRICK

Occasionally, a brick in the middle of a course starts to crumble and has to be replaced. This is how:

1. Chip out the brick and the mortar surrounding it, clean the cavity of any loose chips and spray water into it to dampen the surface.
2. Spread a layer of mortar over the bottom of the cavity. Dampen the replacement brick, spread mortar over its top surface and sides and slide it into the cavity off a piece of board.
3. Ensure the brick is lined up with its companions, adjusting the amount of mortar as necessary. Use a tuck pointer or jointer to smooth the mortar and finish.

PLASTERING – NOT AS DIFFICULT AS YOU THINK

Plastering a wall is one of those tasks many people think are beyond them. It's not. The golden rule is: you don't have to push the mix against the surface as though your life depended on it. It needs a gentle touch.

1. Make up a stiff plaster mix and brush a liquid bonding agent on the surface to be plastered. Then apply the first layer of plaster, about 10 mm thick, using a float or finishing trowel. Use smooth upward sweeps of the trowel to apply the plaster – and you don't have to push it on, just use an even pressure. Start at the base of the wall and work your way to the top.
2. Smooth and score this first layer with a series of scratches a few millimetres deep. This roughening of the surface will enable the top layer of plaster to adhere to the first layer. Keep the layer damp for 48 hours by wetting it lightly with a fine spray from a garden hose, or cover the area with a plastic sheet.
3. Now apply the final layer. Apply it to a level above the desired one, and screed it with the edge of a straight length of timber. Use a side-to-side movement while pulling the timber down the wall. This removes the high points, and shows you where more plaster is required.
4. Keep on screeding and filling until you have a uniform surface. Finish the job by smoothing the surface using a finishing trowel or float.
5. Now stand back and congratulate yourself.

Chip out the crumbling brick and clear the space of debris.

Slide the brick off a board and into position.

Use smooth, upward strokes to apply plaster.

Smooth and then score this first layer.

This action removes the high points and shows up depressions.

Two lengths of wood clamped to a wall as shown are a useful aid.

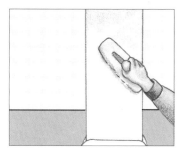

Smooth the final surface to end the job.

An old envelope or a piece of paper folded as shown and taped to the wall minimises mess.

A little squeeze – and you'll clear it with ease.

AND TO END IT ALL . . .

Repairing the plaster on the end of a wall is also easy.

1. Plaster the sides where damaged, and place a length of timber over each so that their edges are in line with the existing plaster. Hold them in place either with a couple of sash clamps or two hoops made up from two reinforcing rods.
2. Now plaster the wall between them, after which you can carefully remove them.
3. The end of the wall can now be smoothed and finished, using a corner trowel if necessary.

NO MESS, WITH JUST ONE SUCK

■ Before drilling into a masonry wall, make up a catcher as pictured, and tape it to the wall below the spot you're drilling – you'll keep mess to a minimum.
■ And to clear dust from the drilling operation from the hole, make up our simple bottle vacuum. Attach a length of aquarium air pipe to the cap of a two-litre plastic cool-drink bottle. Squeeze the bottle, insert the pipe into the hole, and allow the bottle to return to its normal shape – it will take up the dust in the process.

LADDERS

DON'T GET THAT SINKING FEELING

Stop a ladder's feet sinking into the ground, and keep it firm:

1. Drive a stake into the ground between the foot of the ladder and the wall.
2. Lay a piece of scrap chipboard or a short plank on the grass as a rest for the ladder's feet.
3. Now position the latter on the wood and loop a length of rope around the stake in the ground and the bottom ladder rung. The rope will stop the ladder moving under your weight, and the grass below the feet will be unmarked.

A ROUGH ANSWER TO SLIPPERY STEPS

1. Mask off the upper half of each rung of a ladder or a stepladder's steps with masking tape for a neat edge, and apply paint to each area.
2. While the paint is still wet, sprinkle building sand over it quite liberally and allow to dry.
3. Add a second coat of paint and another layer of grit, and you will have created very effective nonslip surfaces.

NOTE: As an alternative to paint and grit, use contact adhesive to stick a strip of coarse sandpaper onto each rung or step.

MIRRORS AND PICTURES

FOIL THAT TARNISHING!

You can disguise unsightly damage to the silvering on a mirror simply by using kitchen aluminium foil. Remove only as much of the damaged or tarnished silver as necessary and apply a piece of foil, shiny side to the mirror, over the damage. It won't stand up to close scrutiny, but will disguise the damage until you can have the mirror properly resilvered.

MIRRORS, HERE'S LOOKING AT YOU

If your favourite antique mirror needs resilvering but the budget won't allow it, have a new mirror cut to the same size and shape as the antique. Scrape the silvering off the latter, taking care not to scratch the glass, and remount it in its frame with the new mirror behind it.

Bear in mind, however, that if your antique mirror is in a frame, which is also an antique, and you have to increase the depth of the rebate to accommodate the new mirror, you could reduce its value. If this is the case, it may be better to wait until you can stretch your budget to have the mirror resilvered professionally.

Moreover, remember that the second mirror will add weight to the whole unit, so you might have to strengthen its attachment setup.

TAPING THAT BATHROOM PROBLEM

One of the hassles with bathroom mirrors is the tarnishing that sometimes occurs around the mirror tape that has been used to fix the mirror in position. And condensation droplets pooling on the top edge of the tape often cause the trouble.

You may still get the problem, but you can extend the life of the mirror if you apply the tape at an angle of about 45 degrees so that moisture cannot pool on any edge.

CLEVER USES FOR MIRRORS

A mirror with all the angles
Mount a small mirror on a length of dowel when you need to look around in areas that would normally have you on your hands and knees – or up a ladder, when you're looking for the ball in the gutter, for instance.

Let there be light
When you cannot get a torch into a tight spot, use a mirror to redirect light to where you need it. And as an added bonus, depending on the angle, you'll be able to see along the reflected beam and spot what you're looking for.

HINT

Using mirrors instead of glass in doors comprising glass panes from top to bottom, helps to create a sense of space.

Because the mirrors are mounted in a door, they give the impression of being a window into the next room.

Getting pictures or mirrors to hang exactly where you want them can be a real challenge! Using this very simple aid (see p. 54) ensures success – every time.

FRAME IT!

A picture frame will often set off the subject it surrounds, enhancing the whole effect; likewise, a large, framed mirror will add depth to a room. This explains why framing is such a successful business. So why not get into it yourself – if only for the satisfaction you will get from making up your own frame.

This is how to make up a frame for a mirror; the basic principles also apply to framing a painting.

1. Select and rout the frame's rebate for the mirror and backing, and do any routing of the other areas of the timber. You will find it easier to rout the entire length of timber in one piece, rather than cutting it into the required lengths and then routing each one individually.
2. Measure each length and mitre each corner join. Remember that the measurement that applies is the inner edge of the rebate, not the inner edge of the frame, because the mirror and backing rest in the rebate. Cut to the inner edge of the frame itself and your frame will be too large. It's a good idea to put the frame together at this stage and check that the backing, and hence the mirror, is a proper fit.
3. Use your drill to make the holes for two dowels in each join.
4. Assemble the frame using two dowels on each corner and glue to secure each join – placing the backing in its rebate will ensure that you have a perfect fit.
5. Once the glue has cured, sand down each join and apply the finish of your choice.
6. Use mirror clips to fix the mirror and backing in position in the frame. Secure the completed unit in position.

Rout the entire length of timber before cutting.

Mitre each corner.

Two dowels secure each mitred join – accuracy is crucial when drilling these holes.

Tape each corner to prevent excess glue marring the surface.

Frames of weathered wood with a nautical touch – perfectly suited to the subject.

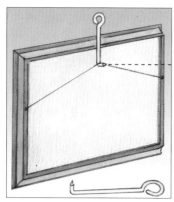

This handy helper makes sure that you hang every picture at exactly the right height.

HANG IT!

One of the challenges – and frustrations – of hanging pictures next to each other is getting them level. But not any more.

1. Take a length of stout wire and make up the aid pictured here. It should be about 150 mm long, so you'll need to use a length of wire of about 200 mm. Bend one end into a circle so that you can grip the aid securely. The other end is sharpened and bent through a right angle.
2. Now all you have to do is to hook the aid over the picture's cord with the point facing the wall. Position the painting as desired and push gently over the point (not too hard, otherwise you could break the glass).
3. Now unhitch the painting and look for the mark on the wall made by the point. And that's where the hanger goes into the wall.

Just one note of caution: support the picture during the exercise – the cord could slip off the aid.

SOUNDPROOFING

QUIET!

Neighbours tend to get upset when they're awoken at a restful hour with the noise of a power tool, lawnmower, or whatever. So the first and simplest rule is not to make a racket when people around you are trying to sleep.

If you feel you have to make a noise, the second rule is to reduce the sound as much as you can – and that's not too difficult, though you won't eliminate it totally.

Sound will get through any gap, so seal gaps as much as you can. Use self-adhesive foam tape to seal gaps around doors and windows. The tape is actually designed to exclude draughts, but it also reduces sound.

DOUBLE YOUR GLASS, HALVE THE NOISE

This might be overdoing it – until the neighbour complains.

So, as prevention is better than cure, frame a piece of glass or Perspex large enough for a garage or workshop window and fix it to the wall, sandwiching foam rubber draught-excluder tape between the frame and the wall.

The double layer of glass is quite effective in reducing the sounds of power tools.

AND WHAT ABOUT THE FAMILY?

Noisy neighbours are annoying, but what about appliances in your own home?

Hard surfaces reflect sound, while foam, carpets and other fibrous materials deaden it. So . . .

This can reduce noise even more and it's hinged so you can open it and let in fresh air when necessary.

- A kitchen appliance can make a lot of noise – until you put it on a sheet of foam (just make sure that you do not block any ventilation vents, otherwise you could cause the motor to overheat).
- Lay carpets or rugs on suspended wooden floors. You may still hear the creak (see elsewhere for the remedy) as a person walks across the floor, but the fibre of the rug or carpet will deaden the sound of the footsteps.
- Put a piece of foam against a wall behind a TV or stereo – this will deaden the sound permeating the wall to the room on the other side. As in other applications, ensure that the ventilation vents on the TV or stereo are well clear so that the set does not overheat.

PLANTING AN IDEA IN YOUR MIND

Plants – trees, bushes, hedges, shrubs, and any other plant you can think of – are not that effective in reducing the sound of passing traffic, even though you may think so. Use them to reduce the impact of strong winds, for instance in the Western Cape, but use a solid wall to reduce the sound of passing traffic. Even then, the wall needs to be high enough to block the direct line between your ear and the source of the noise. You'll need to make a decision – do you cut the noise but accept less of a breeze in your garden, including turbulence from any wind as it swirls over the wall, or do you accept a bit more noise and enjoy a cooling breeze through the garden?

SCISSORS

BENT BLADES?

The blades on scissors sometimes get bent. If bent outwards, they won't cut properly; if bent inwards, they will tend to jam and soon become blunt. So the trick is to bend them back to parallel. To achieve this, put each blade between three blocks of wood in a vice, as shown in the illustration, and gently apply pressure. You may need to repeat the process a few times before you get the right result.

JUST A LITTLE TAP OR TWO

The pivot point of a pair of scissors is sometimes a screw or a bolt, or a rivet, and they sometimes work loose.

- In the case of a screw or bolt, tighten it to the required degree, allowing free movement but no play at the pivot point. Then take a small metal punch and tap the edge of the screw or bolt thread – in the case of the latter, where the bolt and nut meet. This will jam the thread slightly, preventing movement of the screw or bolt in the thread.
- In the case of a rivet, you will need to exercise more caution. Place the scissors on a metal surface and tap the rivet head with a hammer. Check after each tap, and continue until the pivot is tighter, with no play, but still allows free movement.

HINT
Don't plant those young saplings or slips of bushes too close to a wall or the side of the house. Consult your nurseryman for expert advice, but generally don't plant anything that will grow large, closer than 1,5 m to a wall or house. Prune diligently until the trunk is clear of the wall or house.

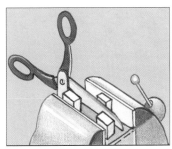

Take care when adjusting a pair of scissors' blades. Bend a little, check a lot!

PLUMBING

CLEARING A DRAIN? SOME CAUSTIC COMMENTS

The outflow pipe for a kitchen sink can become blocked with grease and fragments of food dislodged from plates and dishes. Shower and bath outlets also become blocked, with hair and soap deposits.

In both cases, prevention is better than cure. So try this (you will need protective rubber gloves and a second pair of hands, also protected by gloves):

1. Sprinkle a tablespoonful of caustic soda granules into a sinkful of hot water and leave it to stand for a few minutes while the granules dissolve. Make up a bung from a plastic shopping bag, and have your helper pull out the sink plug.
2. Wait a few moments and, before the solution reaches the outlet, block it with the bung – if you timed everything well, the entire length of the drain, from sink to outside drain, will be full of the hot caustic soda solution.
3. Leave to stand for a few minutes, topping up the sink with hot water if necessary, then remove the bung. The solution will have loosened deposits in the drain and these will be washed out.
4. Repeat, if necessary, and use the same technique for showers, baths and basins.

AROUND THE BEND

Just about everyone has at some time or other dropped something into a toilet, or a child has knocked a toy into it. Put a plastic bag over your hand and retrieve the article, which should then be thoroughly washed and disinfected.

BLOCKED? USE A BUCKET

More modern flushing systems allow you to control a toilet's flush – it saves water. Other versions do not, however, and once the flush has begun, you are committed. The problem in the latter case comes when a toilet has been blocked and you think – and hope – that your efforts to clear the blockage have been successful.

Nothing ruins your day quite like flushing in confidence – and watching the pan fill . . . and overflow. So, if your toilet system is one of the latter, use a bucket to clear the blockage. The sudden force of water is harder than the normal flush, and you can stop it any time you like.

FLUSHED WITH SUCCESS

We live in a country where water is precious, and a toilet in normal daily use takes a lot of water. A good water-saver is a plastic cool-drink bottle filled with water – it displaces its own volume – and two litres saved with every flush adds up. If you find a 2-litre bottle displaces too much water and the toilet is not flushing well, substitute it with a 1,5- or even a 1-litre bottle. Just make sure you position it where it won't interfere with the cistern's operation.

The telltale clues that tell you a toilet cistern fall-valve washer or diaphragm needs replacing are the constant hiss of water going into the cistern and a steady drip from the overflow pipe.

Geysers use the same system, so the sound of your geyser constantly filling – so you think – and water dripping from the overflow pipe are also telltale clues.

REPLACING A BALL-VALVE WASHER IN A CISTERN

1. Turn off the water supply to the cistern – the stopcock is usually mounted on the wall or inlet pipe to one side of the unit.
2. Remove the cap, if there is one.
3. Close the ends of the split pin that acts as a pivot for the float arm, and remove it.
4. Manoeuvre the arm free, using it to pull the piston towards the end of the cylinder as you do so.
5. Remove the piston. [**Hint:** You have to be careful not to damage it, so if you cannot grip it with a pair of pliers, push it back in, put the lid back on the cistern, and then turn the tap on for a second on two. The jet of water is often enough to push the piston out far enough for you to get a good grip on it.]
6. While the piston is out, use a little fine sandpaper on a length of dowel to remove any deposits in the cylinder. If the piston itself is brass, clean it as well if necessary. You can also drape some cloth over the end of the cylinder and turn the water back on for a few seconds – not strongly, but enough to push any dirt out. The cloth will stop the water blasting out all over the bathroom and words being said!
7. Pry the washer out of its recess in the head of the piston and insert the replacement.
8. Position the washer with the slot for the float arm facing directly downwards, and insert it into the cylinder.
9. Gently manoeuvre the float arm in position – which you will be able to do only if the slot in the piston is positioned correctly. [**Hint:** You will find it easier to position the float arm properly if you flush the toilet beforehand – if it's still full of water, the float will tend to make things difficult.]
10. Reinsert the split pin, and spread the ends slightly with a screwdriver blade to prevent its falling out.
11. Turn the water back on and raise the float arm, checking that the water coming into the cistern stops flowing.
12. It does? Nice work!

Remove the split pin, float arm and piston.

Pry the old washer out with a screwdriver and replace it with the new one.

Making sure the piston is positioned with the slot downwards, reinsert it into the cylinder, reposition the float arm and secure with the split pin.

Remove the large knurled nut holding the float arm in position.

Pry the diaphragm out and replace with the new one.

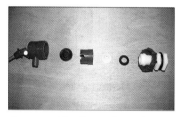

Reassemble the unit and turn on the water. This exploded view shows the component parts.

13. Incidentally, if you find the water in the cistern does not come up to the same level as before, it's because the new washer is a little thicker than the old one where it meets the nozzle. If necessary, bend the float arm up a little so that the float can rise higher and fill the cistern to the required level. Later on you may need to bend the arm down again, as the washer is indented where it meets the nozzle.

NOTE: **If, having replaced a washer or diaphragm, you find the water still flows, the nozzle may need to be replaced. And that's just as easy.** Take the unit apart again, remove the nozzle and if it is damaged, take it down to your local hardware shop for a replacement.

REPLACING A DIAPHRAGM

1. Turn off the water supply and remove the large knurled nut holding the float arm in position.
2. Pry the diaphragm away from the nozzle with a screwdriver.
3. Take the opportunity to clean the unit.
4. Then drape a piece of cloth over the end of the cylinder and turn the water on for a few seconds to remove any dirt.
5. Insert the new diaphragm and replace the knurled nut. Tighten it by hand, firmly, but not so tight that removing it again becomes a problem.

CAUTION

In the case of a geyser repair, turn off the main electrical supply as well as the water mains. What you're doing has nothing to do with the electrical system, but one precaution too many is better than one too few. You might also consider running the hot-water tap for a while before doing the work, so that the water in the geyser is cooler. Replacing the necessary parts is a simple job, however.

NO-STRAIN STAIN REMOVAL

A toilet pan sometimes develops unsightly surface stains made up of deposits of calcium or lime. Use a round-ended knife or putty knife to get rid of the worst of the deposits (gently, so that you don't mark the enamel), then get rid of the remains with a plastic scourer and scouring powder.

REPLACING A TOILET SEAL

The plastic collar that fits over the large toilet outlet pipe might perish after a number of years. Replacing it with the same sort of item is impossible without lifting the toilet off its foundations, so don't. Simply buy the purpose-made substitute, a seal made of dense foam rubber, which is designed to fit tightly into the gap between the larger drain and smaller-diameter toilet outlet. Make sure when installing the seal that the ends meet at the top, otherwise you could find it leaks.

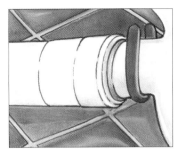

Make sure the new seal is positioned with ends uppermost.

Versatile vinegar – from great-tasting chips to spotless windows – and a descaled kettle element.

VINEGAR, MULTITALENTED, AND GOOD ON CHIPS TOO!

Vinegar is great with fish and chips, but it's more useful than you might have thought:

- Scaly kettle? Scaly iron? Just fill them with a 50/50 mix of water and white vinegar. In the case of the kettle, boil the mix in it and allow it to stand overnight. Rinse out the next day with clean water and celebrate with a cup of tea. And the iron? Steam the mixture until the tank is dry, refill it with clean water and drain it through the steam holes.
- Be a good egg – to stop the white of an egg spreading too far when poaching it, add a tablespoonful of vinegar to the water.
- Dirty collar? Get rid of the grime with a paste of vinegar and bicarbonate of soda rubbed into the stain.
- Oh, those aching muscles . . . or itching skin for that matter! Add half a cup of cider vinegar to your bath, lie back and relax.
- Brush up that brush: you can revive a tired paintbrush by soaking it in a solution of white vinegar and water. Leave it to soak for a few hours, then wash the brush in detergent and allow to dry.
- Rust, begone! Clean a rusted bolt by soaking it in a solution of vinegar for a few days. The rust should dissolve.
- Hair today, shinier tomorrow: dark hair will end up much shinier when you rinse it in a solution of two parts water to one part vinegar. Then, just so that you keep your friends, rinse out well with clean water.
- White, bright, light . . . you'll brighten up your whites by soaking them in 5 litres of warm water to which you have added a cup of white vinegar. You'll also have the bonus of getting rid of detergent residues. Finish by rinsing the items well in clear water.
- Vinegar, clearly the best . . . Just two tablespoonfuls of vinegar in a litre of warm water will give you great results when you clean your windows.

Turn the water off, open the tap and remove the grip and cover, if there is one.

Remove the tap assembly and replace the old washer with a new one.

Reassemble the tap.

Tape stops the drill bit skidding over the tile's surface.

REPLACING A TAP WASHER

Replacing a tap washer is one of those chores that needs doing periodically in every household and, like most other chores, it's easy once you know how.

1. Turn off the water supply and open the tap to allow the water pressure to drop.
2. Remove the grip and then the bell-shaped cover, if the tap is this sort.
3. Remove the tap assembly.
4. Remove the washer from its seating – you may need to remove a small nut to do so.
5. Slip the new washer onto the threaded shaft and replace the nut. Screw it down only enough to hold the washer firmly – you don't have to drive it through the latter!
6. Screw the tap assembly back into place and use a spanner to tighten it. Make sure it is firm, but do not overtighten.
7. Replace the bell-shaped cover, if the tap is this sort, and then the grip.
8. Turn the tap off, and then turn the water supply back on.
9. Turn the tap on and off a couple of times to ensure it is operating properly.
10. Make sure the rest of the household knows that the tap has a new washer and needs only moderate force to turn it off. If you don't, they'll continue using brute force to turn it off and you'll be replacing the washer again – sooner than you think.

NOTE: To avoid marring the chromed tap cover, cushion the spanner with cloth or rubber. You should also put the plug in the drain to prevent the loss of any small part you might drop.

TILE TRICKS

DRILLING INTO THAT TILE
Drilling into a ceramic tile is simple – just follow a few rules.

- First of all, to prevent the drill bit skidding all over the surface, place some masking tape over the spot you're going to drill.
- Secondly, do not use the drill's hammer function until you are through the tile and into the wall; you could shatter the tile.
- Equally important, do not apply a great deal of pressure while going through the tile – again, you might crack it.
- Once into the wall, switch to the hammer function and drill to the required depth.

REPLACING THAT BROKEN TILE
Again, no mystery.

1. Since the tile is broken anyway, break it up into small pieces and clean out the hole it leaves – remove all the adhesive and grouting.
2. Apply a layer of adhesive as close as possible to the level used to seat the surrounding tiles.
3. Now – and this is the clever part – lay a length of cord across the position the tile will take and gently press the tile in position. If you've got the amount of adhesive right, the tile will be level with its companions.
4. Withdraw the cord, wait for the adhesive to dry, and grout.

NOTE: If you need to add adhesive, or remove any, the cord will allow you to lift the tile, adjust the amount and relay it.

HAVE A NIBBLE
For a really neat finish shape tiles to surround plumbing fixtures.

1. Mark the cut line with a wax crayon or felt-tip pen and use a pair of tile nippers to remove small pieces of the tile. If you try to take too big a bite, you're likely to have the tile fracturing at a tangent – so little is more, in this case.
2. Once you get close to your cut line, reduce the amount of each 'bite' further, and finish by sanding the tile to the cut line.

The tile's cracked, so break it out with a chisel.

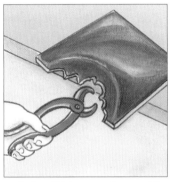

The cord allows you to pull the tile up again and adjust the amount of adhesive, if you have to.

A little nibble at a time, with filing and sanding to finish along the cut line.

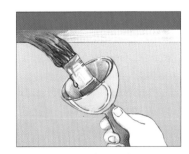

Prevent paint from dripping over your hand.

ANYONE FOR TENNIS? HAVE A BALL!
Apart from the common use of a tennis ball as a covering for the ball on a tow hitch, there are a few more uses which were never considered by the manufacturers!

On guard!
A tennis ball shoved over the end of a sharp-pointed workshop tool or garden implement will prevent injury from the point.

No more scratches
Moving a heavy piece of furniture? A tennis ball shoved over each leg will prevent scratches to wooden floors.

Putting the fun back into painting
When using a paintbrush upside down (the brush, that is – not yourself!), slipping half a tennis ball over the handle will prevent paint dripping down and over your hand – something that takes all the fun out of painting.

Blow it!
Make a small hole in a tennis ball and glue a plastic pipe or nozzle into it, and you'll have a handy blower to get rid of dust in computer keyboards and the like.

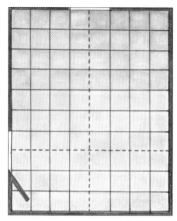

Your focal points are the door and window, so the centres of each are the starting points.

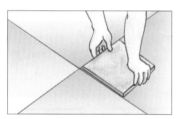

The starting point for laying the tiles is where the lines cross – these are the four possible positions for the first tile. Make sure you lay this extremely accurately – if you're out on this, all your other tiles will be out as well.

Lay pyramid fashion from the centre, working outwards to the walls, where the edging tiles are trimmed as necessary to complete the job.

LAYING TILES . . . A FEW POINTERS

For best visual impact, your tiles need to be 'in balance' around the focal point of the room – a doorway, for instance. Mark out your primary baseline, running down the middle of the room, along the longest axis. Then, in this case, as the door is the focal point, mark a line at right angles to the first, from the middle of the door opening to the far wall. Then begin laying the tiles, starting where the two lines meet in the middle of the room.

The view from the door once the tiling is complete should be one of balance.

MEASURING MADE EASY

FIND THE CENTRE, MR VENTER

There are two methods to find the centre of a circular sheet of wood or metal, when you might wish to attach a post to the centre to make a table, for instance.

1. For larger-diameter items, place a straight length of timber against the rim of the item. Place a second piece of timber at right angles to the first so that it too touches the rim of the item. Finally, a third length of timber is positioned on the other side of the circular item. The centre of the item is on a line from the midpoint between the two parallel lengths of timber. Draw a short line in approximately the centre of the item, turn it through 60 degrees or so, and repeat the procedure. To check, repeat a third and last time: all three lines should meet at the same point – and that is the exact centre of the item.

2. The second method is suitable for smaller items. Clamp a rule to a try square at an angle of 45 degrees and place this contraption on the item to be checked, with both arms of the try square touching its rim. Draw a short line along the rule set at 45 degrees. Turn the item through about 60 degrees, repeat and, as above, repeat a third and final time – where the lines intersect marks the centre.

1

2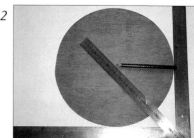

'ONE-NINTH OF 250 MILLIMETRES IS . . . AH, FORGET IT!'

Measuring off segments or strips when the intervals are not a whole number can be a brainteaser – until you try this.

1. Simply lay a rule across the piece to be cut into segments or strips so that the length on the rule is easily divisible by the number of segments or strips. In this example the rule is set to 270 millimetres. Mark the material at 30-millimetre intervals, and repeat at the other end of the timber.
2. Draw the cut lines between the corresponding marks and start cutting.

HOW DEEP?

An ordinary nut and bolt make a handy, accurate way of measuring the depth of a hole. Turn the nut up the bolt, place the end of the latter in the hole and turn the nut down until it reaches the surface. Simple!

BUT IS IT SQUARE?

Make sure that a frame or drawer is absolutely square by measuring diagonally from corner to corner. If the readings are the same, the item is square.

LET THERE BE LIGHT

To check if an edge is straight, hold a rule against it and hold it up to the light. Any light shining through will show you any low areas. When no light is showing, you have a perfect edge.

PYTHAGORAS WAS RIGHT ON THE ANGLE

For measuring a right angle over a longer distance, measure off a large triangle in multiples of 3, 4 and 5 – 900 mm, 1 200 mm and 1 500 mm. The corner opposite the longest side is exactly 90 degrees.

AN ALL-ROUND ANSWER

Marking equal distances around a tube or round post is easy with a length of paper.

1. Wrap it once around the post and make a mark where the end meets the overlap.
2. Now lay the paper out flat – the distance from the end to the mark is the exact circumference.
3. Use a compass or rule to mark the points at equal distances on the paper. Place it around the workpiece again and transfer the marks.

WATER DOWN THAT SWING

Using a plumb bob on a windy day can be a problem if it swings about, making an accurate reading difficult. Use a bucket of water to stop the swing, but ensure the weight is hanging freely in the water and not touching the bucket's side or bottom.

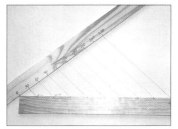

The 'lines' from the rule to the workpiece must be parallel to each other.

A bolt with nut attached makes a handy measure to check the depth of a hole.

Marking equidistant points on the circumference of a pipe or cylinder is easy like this.

This handy helper is a great help when you wish to mark the middle of a length of material.

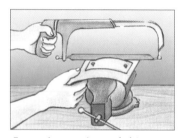

Fastening a piece of thin metal over a curved surface enables you to cut out the centre neatly and accurately.

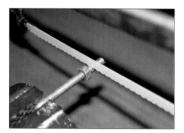

No more problems aligning the thread. Slip a nut on first, cut the bolt and remove the nut – and the thread's aligned. Simple!

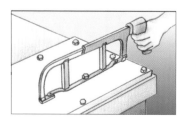

Two inserts push the blade down for a flush cut.

MARK THE MIDDLE, WITHOUT MEASURING

To find the midpoint of a piece of material without measuring is easy. Just make up the item shown. You'll need a scrap piece of wood, two bolts and a pencil.

1. Drill a hole for the pencil in the dead centre of the wood, and then very accurately drill a series of holes for the bolts on either side and along the same line. These holes must be positioned accurately.
2. The pencil goes into the centre hole, and the bolts pass through the holes on either side of the pencil – select the holes to best suit the width of the material to be marked.
3. With both bolts snug against the edges of the workpiece, the pencil point will be dead centre. Draw the centre measure along the workpiece.

MAKING THE RIGHT CUT

CUTTING COMMENTS, SAW POINTS

There is a wide variety of saws on the market. Each type has a number of applications, but there are certain techniques that will help you achieve the desired result, whatever type you're using, and on whatever material.

■ Cutting thin metal can be difficult if the metal is not supported. It will distort and you won't get a clean cut. Clamp the workpiece between two pieces of wood. Mark your cut line on the wood and cut through it, the metal and the lower piece of scrap. The wood supports the metal and prevents distortion.
■ Need to cut a square or rectangle out of a sheet of thin metal? Bend the sheet over a smoothly curved piece of wood (such as a large-diameter fence post) and clamp it firmly into position. Cut through the curve on each end, almost to the corner of the cutout, then turn the sheet through 90 degrees and repeat the process on the last two sides. All that remains is to complete the cuts to each corner carefully.
■ One of the problems with cutting a bolt is aligning the thread afterwards. Just thread a nut onto the bolt first, cut it to length and smooth the cut end with a metal file. Now turn the nut off the bolt – as you do so, it will align the thread.
■ Yes, you can cut off a bolt or dowel flush with the surface. Turn the hacksaw blade horizontal and insert two wood spacers, just long enough to push the blade clear of its attachment points. Now only the cutting part of the blade will lie flat on the surface.
■ You can reduce the chipping of veneer and surfaces such as Formica when you cut them. Score along the cutting line with a sharp blade and cut on the outside of this line. You can even avoid chipping on the scrap side by scoring a second line a millimetre

from the first and cutting between the two. Use the same technique when cutting plywood, and in both applications, if you are using a jigsaw with pendulum or orbital action, set the control to zero – it reduces the ripping effect of the blade.

Trimming a sliver off the end of some timber is easier like this.

- Trimming a sliver of wood off the end of a length of timber? Clamp the workpiece between two scrap pieces with plenty of overlap and saw through all three; the scrap will keep the blade true.
- When you're cutting long lengths with a jigsaw or circular saw, a straight length of timber clamped to the workpiece will keep the power tool straight. If you're in doubt as to setting the correct gap between the cut line and the guide, cut a notch where you should start, place the power tool blade in the notch and then clamp the guide in position.
- Get the angle right. When cutting a piece of angle iron, clamp the workpiece in a vice with the heel uppermost, and cut from there – you will get a far more accurate cut.
- Quiet, please. When you cut steel, brass or aluminium that you have clamped in a bench vice, the free end can make a racket, which you can dampen by draping some cloth over it.

Clamp a guide to the workpiece for an accurate cut.

WELL DRILLED

TAKE A TUBE
One of the challenges of drilling through a tube is keeping the drill bit centred on the convex surface, and keeping the tube securely in place.

1. First of all, rout a 'V' channel in two blocks of scrap.
2. Slip a length of dowel into the tube (if necessary, wrap paper around the dowel to make it fit snugly into the tube). This will reduce the chance of distortion of the tube when it's in the vice.
3. Now place a block on either side of the tube and clamp it into the jaws of the vice. The dowel reduces distortion and the blocks keep the tube right where you want it without marking it.
4. Now comes the clever part. Place a third block of scrap on top of the tube, ensuring that it fits snugly into the space between the two blocks.
5. Drill through the third block and through the tube – the former will keep the drill bit centred on the tube, **provided it fits snugly between the two blocks clamping the tube**. The looser the fit, the less accurate the result.

Drilling through the tube this way keeps the bit where you want it.

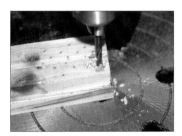

Distortion around the drill hole is eliminated.

DRILLING THROUGH THIN METAL
Try to drill through thin metal that is unsupported and you will almost always distort it – the drill hole will be at the centre of a depression, and you'll be depressed at the result.

The problem is easily avoided: place the metal between two pieces of scrap wood, clamp them together and drill through all three – you'll be impressed with the result.

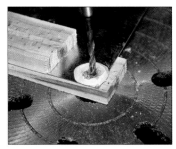

Keeping the drill bit well oiled ensures that it stays sharper for longer.

Make a hole smaller? Glue a dowel into the hole and then drill a hole of the correct diameter.

Make a hole bigger? Clamp the workpiece between two pieces of scrap, and redrill through all three. Easy!

Save those thumbs!

DAM IT!

It's important to keep a drill well lubricated with oil when drilling thicker metals; if the bit gets too hot, it will become blunter more quickly.

So, make a small dam of Prestik or putty around the spot to be drilled and fill it with oil. The drill bit will have a continuous supply of oil and will last longer.

NEED TO MAKE IT SMALLER?

Did you drill a hole that is too large? It happens, but it's simple to fix. If a dowel fits the hole exactly, then miss the next step. If you don't have a dowel that fits the hole, the next step is to drill a hole that will fit a dowel you have.

Cut a slice of dowel to suit the thickness of the wood, apply glue and tap it into the hole you've drilled. Once the glue has set, sand the dowel down flush with the surface, and drill a hole of the required diameter.

NEED TO MAKE THAT HOLE BIGGER?

One of the problems of making a small hole bigger when working with wood, is the lack of purchase the tip of the drill bit has on the wood. This is especially the case when using a spade bit. There are two solutions:

■ Plug the hole with a dowel of the right diameter and drill the hole again.
■ Clamp the workpiece firmly between two pieces of scrap wood and drill through all three – the two scrap pieces above and below the workpiece will keep the bit centred.

NAILS, NUTS AND SCREWS

NAIL THE PROBLEM

Keep those thumbs out of the way – use a piece of folded card or a pair of pliers to hold a nail, particularly when you need to drive it into an awkward spot. No more sore fingers.

PULL IT OUT – WITHOUT DAMAGE

A wedge of wood with a groove cut into it will enable you to remove any nail without damaging the surrounding surface with the hammer, and you will be able to pull the nail out straight.

Pull the nail just far enough so that you can then use the wedge under the hammerhead to pull it out further. Move the wedge progressively further under the hammerhead as the nail is pulled – it will come out straight and can be reused.

LOCK THAT NUT!

- Apply a little hot glue to the thread of a bolt and, while it is still hot and fluid, tighten the nut. The glue will set in the thread and lock the nut tight, but you will still be able to loosen it if necessary.
- A more permanent method of preventing a nut coming loose is to cut through the middle of the bolt as shown, and then spread the halves just enough to prevent the nut loosening. To remove the nut, simply close the halves gently with a pair of pliers.

ROUNDED OFF? CUT IT OUT

Solve the problem of the rounded-off nut like this: cut a segment out of one side to provide a purchase for a spanner or vice grip.

RUSTED? BUILD A DAM

Don't waste that penetrating oil. Build a small dam around the nut with putty or Prestik. It will keep the oil where you need it.

NO SCREWDRIVER? NO PROBLEM!

Clamp an ordinary steel washer on end into the chuck of a brace and use it on a slotted screw head.

GET A GRIP!

You'll improve your grip on a screwdriver handle simply by wrapping a couple of elastic bands around the handle a few times.

TAKE THE TUBE

If you have had a screwdriver blade slip out of the slot and slam into the wood below, join the club.

1. A small tube of the right diameter slipped over the screw head will keep the head of the screwdriver right where you need it. If you don't have a tube of the right diameter, use two nuts. The first one should be a reasonable fit on the head of the screw, so that it can be screwed onto the head for at least a turn or two.
2. Once you get close enough to the surface below, remove the nut and drop one of a larger diameter over it. It should be large enough to drop freely over the head of the screw. Now drive the screw home completely.

MAKING A SPECTACLE OF IT

If you lose the tiny screw that joins one of the hinges on your spectacles, use a small paper clip as a temporary repair. Open it out partly into the shape of a P and slide the leg of the P into the hole for the screw, with the rest of the clip on the outside of the earpiece. Then bend the leg back up to the outside so that the entire clip is clear of your eye. It doesn't look pretty, but should last until you can have the screw replaced.

Here's a sure way to stop a nut working loose.

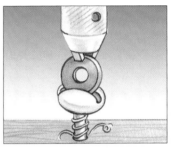

No screwdriver? Slip a washer into a brace and use that. It works. No washer? Try a coin.

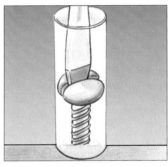

A tube keeps the blade where you want it – in the slot.

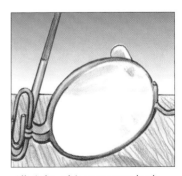

All right, this may not look good – but it works.

Wrap the bristles in a few centimetres of newsprint and secure it in place with a rubber band over the metal.

The bristles remain neat, which enables you to achieve a neater result.

Remove the door hardware, slip it into a bag and then reattach it. Later, loosen slightly, and tear the bag off.

PAINTING

SUBSTITUTE STRIPPERS

■ Use oven cleaner to strip paint and varnish off less valuable items you plan to paint. Don't use it on more valuable ones, as it will darken the wood. Neutralise the stripped surface with vinegar and wash thoroughly with water.

■ And, like phoenix rising from the ashes, door hardware will be easier to clean of paint or varnish after being soaked in a solution of 250 g wood ash and 10 litres water. Allow it to soak overnight and scrub the paint and varnish residues off in the morning.

■ And there's nothing like milk to resist today's strippers – if it's milk paint from a century or so ago. Ordinary household ammonia will do the job, but think about it first – stripping off the old milk paint and refinishing the piece could well reduce its value. New is not always better!

KEEP YOUR PAINTBRUSH IN THE NEWS

To stop paintbrush bristles splaying after cleaning, roll a strip of newspaper around the brush after cleaning. It will keep the bristles in line and doesn't slow the drying process, as it allows the water to evaporate.

DON'T HAVE A HARD TIME PAINTING AROUND HARDWARE

Painting around door hardware need not be a hassle.

■ The easiest and best way to solve the problem is to remove the hardware, or loosen it sufficiently to paint under it and reattach it once the paint has dried.

■ Applying masking tape around hardware works well, but can be a challenge if the hardware is ornate. The alternative is to remove the hardware, slip it into a plastic shopping bag, and reattach it. Pull the bag back tightly so that it is snug against the edge of the hardware, and paint around it. Once the paint is dry, simply pull the plastic bag away (you may need to loosen attachment screws slightly to free the last remnants).

SHORT OF A TRAY FOR A ROLLER?

A roasting tray makes a good substitute – but make sure you cover it well in clingwrap or you will be the one getting the roasting.

STRAIGHT FROM THE CAN

Roller trays don't hold a large amount of paint, so rather load the roller directly from the can. Take a piece of expanded metal screen and bend the ends so that it hangs in the bucket. Roll the roller over it to remove excess paint.

Want to give an old wooden table a new look? Use oven cleaner to strip off the paint quickly and easily!

Three or four holes in the rim allow excess paint or varnish to drip back into the can.

HINT

You can use your nut – a large old one, anyway – to make mixing faster. Drop an old nut into the paint can before you close it the first time. Before opening it again, give it a good shake – the nut will bounce around in the can, stirring the contents up. Naturally, this works with more fluid paints, not the nondrip version.

Properly mixed, a paint product will give you the results you expect. Properly stored, a can of paint can be used repeatedly over a long time and still give you the finish you want.

Feeling lumpy? Just take the strain

Get rid of lumps in paint the easy way with an old pair of pantihose – and make sure they're old; you don't want the silent treatment. Stretch a leg over the top of a can, keep it in place with a rubber band, and pour the paint into a new container. The pantihose's tight weave makes an excellent strainer.

Take a holistic approach to mixing

Make your paint stirrer more effective by drilling holes of about 6-8 mm diameter along the length. As you stir, the paint flows through the holes as well as around the sides of the stirrer and you get better, quicker results.

From pastry to paint

When that kitchen mixer wears out, grab the beater attachment – it makes an excellent paint mixer when mounted on a power drill. But a word of caution: don't remove it from the paint while it is still rotating – the result can be interesting!

A hole in the rim saves paint

Use a nail to make three or four holes in the rim of a paint can. The holes are sealed when the top is in position, but allow excess paint to drip back into the can during use.

You've got to draw the line somewhere

Ever notice how dried paint deposits make it difficult to seat a lid properly? Not any more. Draw a line across one side of the lid and onto the can itself. Align the two every time you close the can and you'll be assured of a tight fit, every time.

Be the first to cross the wire

Use a couple of those holes in the rim, as mentioned above, as seats for a piece of wire across the open top of the can. Wipe excess paint off the brush and onto the wire – it will keep the paint dripping straight back into the can. For convenience, don't put the wire right across the middle, but off to one side so that you have more space in which to insert the brush into the paint.

BROOM! BROOM! EXTEND THAT REACH

Why climb on a ladder when you can reach way up high by pushing the end of a broomstick into the handle of a roller? It's great for doing the upper reaches of walls, ceilings and so on.

WHEN YOU SHOULD PAINT YOURSELF INTO A CORNER

When using a roller to paint a wall, you won't be able to get right into the corners, or paint accurately along the skirting or cornice.

Use a paintbrush to paint these areas first, then use the roller to get in as close as you can. The edge is far less noticeable than if you used the roller first and then the paintbrush – which will give you sharp edges where one method of application has been changed to another.

LET US SPRAY

Spray-painting achieves smooth results, but a couple of techniques will improve your results, for example releasing the trigger for a moment at the end of each pass. If you don't, there is a moment when the sprayer is stationary – and you deliver more paint than you intended. Remember, the object is to deliver a thin, even coat with every pass.

HOLD THAT POSITION

As with many hand tools, getting yourself in the right position is important before you start – otherwise even the smallest shuffle one way or another can ruin the job. This is as important when spraying as in any other task.

So, position your body at the midpoint of the area to be covered, keep it parallel to the surface, and your arm perpendicular to it. Start moving your arm before pressing the trigger and keep an even speed as you swing across the surface. Also ensure that the electrical cord is long enough to allow you to cover the area without coming up short.

BEND IT!

You need to keep the sprayer at the same distance from the surface – about 200 mm and at a right angle to it, so bend your wrist as you spray.

A GOOD TECHNIQUE, BAR NONE

Spray-painting is particularly good for rough surfaces and for items such as burglar bars. The problem with the latter is that a good portion of the paint goes straight between the bars and is wasted, so hang a number of burglar bars close together, but not touching, and apply the paint from an extreme angle. You will still have wastage, but you'll notice that you're applying paint to what seems like a solid surface.

HINT
Painting your stairs? First do the left-hand half of every step, from the top of the stairs to the bottom, and instruct everyone to use the right-hand side while the finish dries. Then complete the job on the right-hand side. Just make sure everyone knows when to use which side!

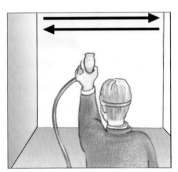

Keep that position and keep the nozzle at right angles to the surface and a constant distance from it.

So that's how it will look.

STAINS AND VARNISH

THE ACID TEST
Before varnishing a surface, get rid of unsightly dark water marks on stripped surfaces with an application of oxalic acid. Wear protective gloves and eye protection, make up a solution with boiling water, and apply it to the mark with a brush. Once the stain has disappeared, neutralise the surface with distilled white vinegar. Check for any differences in the wood's colour while the surface is still wet, and apply stain as necessary.

THAT'S THE SPIRIT!
Wiping a surface with a cloth dampened with mineral spirits will give a good idea of how the surface will look when coated with a clear varnish finish.

JUST A SQUEEZE FOR EASE
Lemon juice is a versatile aid in the home. For instance, you can use it for:

- Lightening your hair – just comb some through your hair and let it dry in sunlight. Do this once a day for a week or so, making sure to use a conditioner between treatments, and after a few days you should start to see a difference in your hair colour.
- Stopping those avocados discolouring, by sprinkling lemon juice over the slices.
- Giving your fingernails a treat, simply by soaking them in a cup of warm water into which you have squeezed the juice from half a lemon.
- Putting the crunch back into your limp lettuce: just soak the lettuce in a bowl of cold water to which the juice of half a lemon has been added and then refrigerate the lettuce for an hour.
- Getting rid of spots: a pimple cannot stand being dabbed with undiluted lemon juice several times a day.
- Cleaning piano keys, with a paste of two parts table salt and one part lemon juice. Wipe off with a damp cloth and finish by polishing with a dry one.
- Keeping apples from turning brown, simply by dipping the cut pieces into lemon juice for a second.
- Giving the air in the home a fresh start after cooking fish: a piece of lemon left in the oven at 150 °C for a quarter of an hour will work wonders.
- Giving your hands a fresh start as well, after cooking fish: just put some mustard in the palm of your hand, add a few drops of lemon juice to make a paste, and rub it into your skin well. Wash your hands in the normal way.
- Giving that sponge a new lease of life: just soak it in lemon juice and then rinse it out well – and voila! A new sponge!

HINT
Keep the stain off your hands – if you don't have rubber gloves, even a plastic shopping bag is better than nothing.

Staining a piece of furniture or timber can give it an entirely new look, but you need to know beforehand that the result you get is the one you want.

A test in time . . .

Before you stain and varnish an entire surface and then decide that the result is definitely not what you wanted, try it on the underside of a table top or in an unobtrusive area of the unit. If you make a mistake, it is less of a disaster than completing the job. Just one point – remember that the underside of a table, for instance, would not have been affected by the sun, so it will tend to have a different colour to the top, which might have been in the sun for long periods.

This sounds quite tacky

The cleaner the surface, the better the result, and an easy way to remove every tiny speck of sawdust or dust from a surface is to use a tack cloth. Dip a piece of cheesecloth or any other lint-free cloth into turpentine and then put a few drops of varnish on it. Knead it a bit to distribute the latter, and then wipe the surface clean in long sweeps from one side to the other. Sweep with the grain so that the cloth's fibres don't get caught on the wood.

Experiment!

The more stain you apply to a surface, the darker it will tend to be. So, use a piece of offcut of the same timber as you intend staining, and apply a stain. Once it is dry, apply a second coat, but leave the last 50 mm or so untouched. Repeat another two or three times, so that you end up with a stepped result – ranging from lightest to darkest. You'll be able to tell at a glance which number of coats suit you best.

Perfect pantihose

Any cloth used to apply stain can leave fibres and lint on the work. So use a pad of old pantihose material. It won't leave lint about and has the added advantage of not absorbing much of the solution, so waste is reduced.

Reaching right into those cavities

Applying an even layer of stain, or any finish for that matter, to ornate surfaces can be a challenge, as a paintbrush's bristles tend to skip depressions and deposit more stain on ridges.

So bring a soft old toothbrush into action. Apply a little heat to the neck of the handle and turn the brush through about 60 degrees. Now you have a handy brush for all those hard-to-reach spots.

HINT
Wood grain – of just about any wood – is most attractive. So, rather than obliterating it with a thick coat of paint, apply a very diluted wash (use water for water-based paints, thinners for oil-based) to add the tinge of your choice to an item of furniture. As always, experiment first – but once you get it right, you'll be pleased with the result.

The more you stain, the darker it gets, so try a stepped test like this, and then choose the number of coats that suit you best.

Any wooden surface requires regular maintenance. The numerous tips under 'Working with wood' will help to ease this task.

WORKING WITH WOOD

SAVE THOSE SANDINGS!

One of the challenges when filling holes in wood is in matching the filler to the surrounding surface. When working on a task, save some of the sandings in a small container – a 35-mm film canister is ideal – and mix them with white filler to obtain a close match. Just remember that varnish will make the mix a bit darker, so allow for this when making up your mix.

THE PLANE TRUTH

There are a few simple techniques that will make planing plain sailing.

Avoid chipping

When you have to plane across the end grain of a piece of wood, the fibres at the end of the wood will splay out as the blade passes over them. The trick is to support them, and the way to do that is to clamp a piece of scrap wood firmly to the end and plane that as well. It will chip away, but it will prevent your workpiece doing so.

A scribble in time . . .

Knowing what you have planed and what you have missed is often difficult – but scribbled pencil marks will show you as you go along exactly where you have planed a surface, and where not.

Keep it straight

Once you are experienced you will find planing, particularly with a power plane, a pleasure. But you can find at times that you might cant the plane a little to one side or the other (the trick is to keep the base plate flat on the surface) and so end up with an uneven surface. This is most likely to happen when planing narrow surfaces, such as the end of a piece of plywood. To prevent this, do the following:

1. Drill a 6-mm hole through a length of scrap to which a second piece of scrap has been fixed, so that the blade of the plane will make contact with the work surface. Firmly attach this guide to the side of the plane with a butterfly nut. It must be at a right angle to the base of the planer. In the case of a jackplane, for instance, simply clamp a piece of wood to the body of the plane opposite the blade.
2. Now plane as usual, ensuring you keep the guide against the side of the workpiece. The plane will stay square.

When planing across the end, clamp a piece of scrap to the end to prevent chipping.

When planing a mitred edge, a scribble or two will tell you when you are nearing the edge.

This simple guide will help you keep a planer exactly level when planing along a narrow edge.

Knots are harder than the surrounding wood, so angle the plane to help the blade slice through the knot.

Convert your sander into a polisher – instantly.

Knot a problem
Being denser than the wood surrounding it, a knot often presents a bit of a problem when planing. The solution is simple – hold the plane at an angle, so that the blade slices through the knot rather than cutting through it.

A closer shave
When planing a surface down to a set of marks, progressively reduce the depth of cut the closer you get to them. This ensures you won't go deeper than planned. Good planers allow you to adjust the depth of cut – so do so.

NEED TO DO A LITTLE POLISHING? GET WEAVING
Convert your sander into a polisher instantly – simply put a piece of cloth between the sanding pad and the surface, switch on the sander and start polishing. The paper's grit grabs the cloth's fibres, which in turn prevent the grit from touching the surface. So it's a win-win situation.

PRESERVE THOSE POSTS!

Wooden posts are exposed to all sorts of conditions – from foul weather to fungi to insects – so their preservation is a matter of some concern.

COLOUR-CONSCIOUS
- When you wish to preserve the wood's natural colour, a good choice of preservative is boron or tributyltin oxide-lindane (TBOL).
- If you don't mind its becoming a little darker, then you can use pentachlorophenol (PCP) or pentachlorophenol-zinc naphthenate (PCPZN).
- If the wood you're treating will be exposed to rain, incorporate a water repellent with any of these products to prevent leaching.
- Finally, since a greenish tinge can be attractive in certain situations, you can use a copper-chromium-arsenic product, which will give the wood this colour. Since this compound will not leach out of the wood, no water repellent is necessary.

SOAK IT UP
Stand posts in a large drum of creosote for a few days before you set them in their holes, so that the preservative has extra time to soak into the wood. This is much easier than painting it on, and wastage is kept to a minimum.

WRAP IT UP

Put a plastic shopping bag over the end of a post before anchoring it in the ground – the bag will afford the buried section of the post a bit more protection for that much longer.

DRY, VERY DRY

Applying a preservative to wood that is wet or even damp could be a waste of time and money. If in doubt, check the instructions and/or contact an expert.

AND TO TOP IT ALL . . .

The better the top of a post sheds water, or is protected from it, the better. To help it shed water, cut the top at a sharp angle or in the shape of a pyramid.

A lengthier procedure is to cap it, which you may prefer to do in certain situations. A metal cap is one alternative, and a wood one is another. In the latter case, rout a groove around the lower edge, about 5 mm in, so that rainwater won't seep under the cap and into the post.

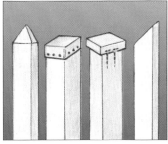

Take care of the tops, too: make sure that they shed rainwater, or are capped.

CAUTION

- Situations vary a great deal, so check with the experts first before deciding upon a preservative. Making the wrong choice can be costly.
- Treat all these products as toxic and take the necessary precautions: wear rubber gloves and safety goggles. An old sweatband is also a useful addition – if you're working on a hot day and start sweating, and any preservative lands in your hair, perspiration could carry it into your eyes. Painful!

Want to know the best way to apply a finish to an ornate surface? Use a soft toothbrush! (see p. 73).

Sanding wood is the key to a great finish at the end of the job – even the planed-all-round timber you buy at your local hardware dealer will need a good sanding if you want a great finish.

TRUE GRIT – BY DEGREES

The rougher the surface, the more grades of sandpaper you may need to go through. They range through the following:

- Coarse – 50 to 60 grit – for removing paint and sanding the roughest surfaces. Also useful when shaping.
- Medium – 80 to 100 – for sanding previously painted surfaces and for use at the intermediate stage of sanding, after rough sanding using 50 or 60 grit paper.
- Fine – 120 to 150 – for final sanding before applying a finish such as paint or varnish.
- Very fine – 160 to 240 – for smoothing primer or paint.
- Extra fine – 280 to 320 – for smoothing between undercoats.
- Superfine – 360 to 400 – for wet-sanding varnish, lacquer or car body paint for an ultrasmooth finish. Using water with this grade has the added advantage of keeping the work surface cool (vigorous sanding can generate sufficient heat through friction to cause certain finishes to start melting).

DON'T GO AGAINST THE GRAIN

Even the slightest scratch from sanding across the grain can be difficult to remove, and the wood's fibres will tend to be lifted more as well. So always sand with the grain.

STOP IT MOVING

It's not always possible to clamp a workpiece into position, but the rubberised base of some bathroom mats is a great nonslip material. So? Staple an old bathmat, nonslip base uppermost (it had better be old; you don't want to have the subject come up at dinner), to a large sheet of plywood or chipboard that can be clamped into position. Now place the workpiece on the rubber base of the bathmat and start sanding. It should stay right where you want it, and there won't be a mark on it.

SANDING A SMALL ITEM? GET A GRIP!

You'll find it easier to move the item over the paper, rather than vice versa, but gripping it can be a problem. Try hot-glueing a short dowel to the back of the item, or put a small piece of mirror tape on the end of your finger, and hold the item that way.

Sand with the grain, not across it.

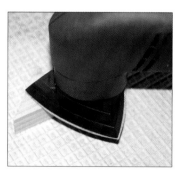

An old bath mat gets a new lease of life when you use it as a nonslip base for keeping a workpiece in one place; very useful when you cannot easily hold the piece in a vice.

THERE'S A BIT OF A FLAP ON . . .

Make your own flap sander from a piece of dowel, some masking tape, and a strip of sandpaper.

1. Make two counterclockwise turns of the tape around the dowel and tape the last 30 mm or so to the grit surface of the sandpaper. This should be long enough to cover the masking tape completely when the paper is wrapped around the dowel.
2. Clamp the dowel in the drill chuck and apply to the workpiece. This little trick works well when you are sanding curved surfaces.

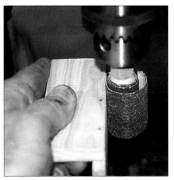

Make your own flap sander – good for smoothing curved surfaces as well.

GET A HANDLE ON UNCLOGGING GRIT

When a sanding disk or pad clogs up, pass the end of the handle of a toothbrush over it while it's on the move. The plastic melts and picks up the debris that is clogging the grit.

MAKE THAT VARNISH VANISH

Know that deposit of varnish or paint that gets deposited on sandpaper when you sand a varnished or painted surface? Most of it will flake off when you run the paper, grit side uppermost, over a sharp edge such as the edge of a piece of wood. Pick the rest off with a knife blade, and carry on sanding.

NINE LIVES

Sandpaper can have more than one life, so as a piece becomes more and more worn, its grit effectively becomes finer, to some extent at least. It's not a good idea to use this paper for tasks in which the finish is of prime importance, but when used for odd jobs such as removing rust from metal or a bit of rough shaping, it helps you save the newer paper for when it really matters.

STAY IN SHAPE – OR PICK A CARD

Sanding a routed surface, a groove, a moulding? The key is to apply equal pressure across the whole surface, so that you do not end up altering its shape.

■ Use a sanding sponge, available from hardware dealers, or use a piece of sandpaper held on a firm bathroom sponge.
■ And when sanding a groove, a length of dowel, pipe or garden hose of a diameter slightly less than that of the groove, works well. A pack of playing cards, held edge on, is another way of staying in the groove.

HINT

Holding a workpiece against a sanding disk continuously will sometimes burn the wood; the trick is to touch it to the disk repeatedly, for a few seconds each time. This way the wood doesn't scorch as a result of the heat caused by friction.

Whether a joint is good or not can determine how strong a wood item may be, to say nothing of how good it will look when complete. Here are a few joints that can be applied in a number of situations. There are others, and variations on these, but the following will meet most applications.

The trick is to practise getting them right and using woodworking aids when these are available. A common factor is this, though: the better the two edges meet, the stronger the joint will be. Secondly, do not use clamping force to make good a joint that is faulty – in time the joint is likely to come apart as the wood tries to return to its natural alignment.

BUTT THIS IS EASIEST

A butt joint, in which the end of one piece of timber meets the other without any further working, is the easiest joint. But it is also one of the weakest, so it needs reinforcing with fasteners such as dowels or biscuits.

Drill the holes for the two dowels into the end of the crosspiece, and corresponding holes into the edge of the piece it is to meet. The combined depth of each hole should be a millimetre or two deeper than the dowel is long, so the edges of the joint can seat properly and there is room for excess glue to accumulate.

A JOINT WITH A DEFINITE EDGE

Edge joints, used to join longer lengths of timber, are strong but, again, strength will be enhanced with dowels or biscuits.

1. To prevent warping, ensure that the two pieces, when joined, will have the grain in alternating directions, so begin by laying them in position and checking the grain.
2. Now drill the dowel holes along the edges to be joined. The holes should be at regular intervals – depending on the length, probably about 200 mm between each.
3. Apply tape along each edge to prevent excess glue marring the surface next to the joined edges. Apply glue to the dowel holes and edges, insert the dowels and put sash clamps top and bottom.
4. Scrap timber across the ends of the workpiece will ensure that the surfaces are aligned.

HALF A LAP IS BETTER THAN NO LAP AT ALL

End-lap or cross-lap joints are used when two pieces of timber cross – the end being on a corner, and the cross being a joint somewhere along the length of the timber.

A butt joint, using dowels or biscuits as reinforcement, is one of the simplest joints – but you must ensure that the holes for the dowels or slots for the biscuits are positioned accurately.

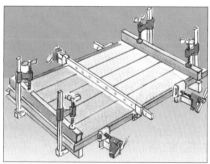

Edge joints are strong but, as always, dowels or biscuits will enhance the strength of the joint.

1. Often, the joint is not good because the depth or width of the cut is too deep. So always cut on the inside of the mark-up lines, and take care to cut to the correct depth. When joining a piece of much thinner cross-section to one that is much thicker, consider making the cutout for the entire depth of the thinner piece in the latter.
2. Accurately mark the cut lines for the width of the joint, and use a marking gauge to mark the depth of the cut. It is crucial that you cut neither too wide nor too deep. On wider joints, make a series of cuts between the outer pair, as this will enable you to chisel out the centre with less risk of too much splintering out.
3. Once the cutouts are finished, dry-fit the pieces together, remove any excess material if necessary, then apply glue and clamp until dry.

MITRES – DIFFICULT, BUT DECORATIVE

Getting consistently good results with mitre joints is rather more difficult than with some other joints, until your skills have matured.

1. Use a mitre box to cut the mitres and dry-fit the two halves to ensure that they match up and present a right-angled joint.
2. Now mark down the centre with a marking gauge, and mark the positions for the drill holes if using dowels to joint the halves. Remember, they must correspond exactly for a good result.
3. If using a block insert across the mitre to strengthen the joint, you will need to clamp the two halves in position and mark the space for the block on the reverse surface. Mark the depth on the inner edge, and carefully chisel out the recess for the block. If using a biscuit jointer, make the seating groove for the biscuit down the centre of the mitred edge.
4. You can strengthen a mitre joint (or any other joint, for that matter) with any of the following:
   Dowels: These can be positioned parallel with one edge, or at a right angle to the mitre, but you will have to take care to ensure that the holes in each half of the mitre correspond exactly.
   Block insert: You would use this on the reverse of a mirror frame or picture frame so that it does not show. A simple square will strengthen the joint, but a double dovetail will lock the two halves of the joint together very positively.
   Biscuit joint: A specialised biscuit jointer is used to make a semicircular groove in the joint and a corresponding groove in the edge of the other half of the joint. The biscuit, wood with an oval section, fits into the two grooves, providing a strong bond and strengthening the joint.

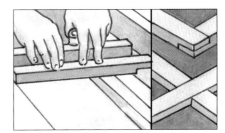

A lap joint is comparatively weak and needs reinforcement if it is to take any heavy load.

A ply insert, biscuit or dowels enhance the strength of one of the neatest joints – the mitre.

It's best to use a jig when dovetailing corners. Skilled carpenters never needed them, but why not take advantage of advances?

THE DOVETAIL

Dovetail joints are amongst the strongest of joints. There are two common versions – that used to join two lengths of timber, such as a strut to a table leg, and that used on the corner of a drawer.

The dovetail on a strut:
1. Cut the dovetail's shoulders and cheek first and lastly the angle, and use it as the template to mark up its housing on the second piece of timber.
2. Carefully make the edge cuts, with an extra cut or two between them for ease of chiselling. Dry-fit the two parts to ensure a tight fit, remove any excess material, then glue and clamp until dry.

The dovetailed corner:
Doweling jigs are available that make this joint much easier to accomplish. The jig is used in conjunction with a router with a dovetail bit and bushing.

1. Practise with a couple of scrap pieces to set the stop screws to the proper offset, and to select the correct spacers for the right depth of cut.
2. Then securely clamp the two workpieces into position and make the first pass with the router from left to right across the tips of the template fingers to reduce the risk of splintering when routing the pins and sockets.
3. Now, ensuring that the bushing on the bit stays in contact with the template fingers at all times, move the router across the doweling jig.
4. Make a second pass in the reverse direction and then remove the pieces from the jig, dry-fit them and, once satisfied with the result, apply glue and complete the join.

THE HOUSING AND STOPPED HOUSING

These joints are commonly used in items such as bookcases, to join shelves to sides, when the shelves will have to bear great loads. Both involve cutting a channel the full thickness of the shelf into the side, to a depth of 5 mm or so.

The housing joint involves the channel going the full width of the timber, while the channel for a stopped housing stops about 20 mm short of what will be the front edge. This will give the finished piece a better appearance.

A router with a straight bit is ideal for cutting the channel for the stopped housing joint, but take care at the ends, where chipping can occur – a short cut with a saw can prevent this.

Alternatively, a radial arm saw or table saw fitting with a dado blade can be used to cut the channel.

Housing and stopped housing joints are often found in bookcases.

In the case of the stopped joint, the front end of the shelf has to be cut back the depth of the channel so that the front edge of the shelf meets the upright neatly.

MORTISE AND TENON

The mortise and tenon is a strong joint used in framework, the trick being to ensure that the tenon – the projecting piece – fits tightly into the mortise – the opening for it.

One way to ensure this is to make two cuts in the tenon a few millimetres in from the edge. A small wedge driven into each of these will force the outer edges of the tenon apart, hard up against the mortise, and ensure a very tight fit.

If the tenon passes right through the mortise, you can drive the wedges in during assembly, before the glue has set. If the tenon does not pass right through, you will need to position the wedges in the cuts, so that they are just held, and then assemble the joint.

As the tenon is pushed into the mortise, the ends of the wedges come up against the bottom of the mortise and are then pushed into their final position, expanding the tenon as they do so.

1. Set a mortise gauge to the desired width of the tenon – usually, depending on the thickness of the timber, about a third of it – and mark the thickness lines on the end of the member. For a better result, allow a little excess length on the latter so that you can trim and finish it for a neat result.
2. Mark the tenon out on the end of the crosspiece and cut the tenon out. If you are going to use wedges as well, make two cuts through the tenon a few millimetres in from each edge.
3. The mortise can be made either by hand with a chisel (the ends of the mortise must be squared with a chisel about 2 mm narrower than the width of the mortise), or by drilling a series of holes. If the latter, use a broad chisel to remove the wood between the holes and smooth the sides of the mortise.
4. Dry-fit the joint to ensure the fit is good and then complete the joint, using glue to secure.

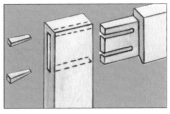

Mortise-and-tenon joints ensure a sturdy frame.

HINT

The looser the joint, the more likely it is to fail. This is true particularly of chairs, because they have to flex and undergo strain as the sitter shifts. So, make every join as tight as you can, without overstressing the wood and causing it to crack. Cut inserts slightly oversize and sand down to the required dimensions. A little sanding will go a long way towards a good join. As you become more skilled, the fit will be better – without the sanding.

TIGHT SITUATIONS

Clamping workpieces together while the glue cures is essential for a good bond, and there are a few tricks of the trade to ensure trouble-free clamping, every time.

1. No marks are good marks – wood buffers like this, made up from thin scrap, will prevent the jaws of your vice marking wood you've secured for shaping, cutting or glueing. When making up the buffers, make sure the screw or nail heads are countersunk.
2. Need to hold a length of wood in place for planing? Two offcuts with a V cut into each and clamped to the bench with the work-piece securely held between them, make the job a lot easier.
3. Don't have a sash clamp, or one of sufficient length? Make one from scrap wood and a couple of wedges. Nail a T-piece across each end, ensuring they are far enough apart to straddle the pieces to be clamped together. You will also need two wedges – it's best if they come from the same piece of wood. Now put your makeshift clamp in position and tap the two wedges in position; as they move together, they exert a pressure on the work surface and the pieces to be glued are pushed together.
4. Have to glue an item to a surface, but it's too far from the edge for your clamp to reach? Try this: lay a piece of scrap between the item to be glued and a block of scrap on the edge of the main surface. Now apply a clamp, as far in as you can, to apply pressure beyond the block to the 'bridge'. The end of that will, in turn, press down on the item to be glued to the surface. Simple!
5. A caulk gun makes a handy clamp to apply light pressure to small pieces of wood.
6. Round surfaces can be a problem when you try to clamp two pieces together – flat clamps provide adequate pressure, but will flatten the rounded surface. So use a hose clamp! They are available in a variety of sizes and are a great help when fixing split chair legs, for instance. As usual, a cushion between the work surface and the clamp is a good idea, so wrap a couple of layers of paper around the leg first.
7. Clamping along the edge of a flat surface, for instance when you're reglueing a veneer, is simplified when you secure a clamp as shown, and then use wood wedges to apply pressure to the edging.
8. Another way to hold a long workpiece is to secure a sash clamp in a vice, and then secure the workpiece in the clamp.
9. Getting chair legs to stay together while glue sets just needs a couple of tiedowns.
10. Substitutes that work: mousetraps work well on smaller pieces that have to be glued, and jumper lead clamps can work for slightly larger pieces.

SOME CLAMPING HINTS

■ Don't use a clamp to apply too much pressure; if you squeeze out too much of the glue, you will reduce the strength of the bond.

■ A bad join is a bad join, and using a clamp to force the pieces into position is simply not going to last.

■ Use hand pressure only to tighten a clamp or vice. Never use a wrench.

■ Leave the clamps on for the recommended time to ensure that the glue has set properly.

■ Do not remove the clamps before the time and begin painting or varnishing the item. If the glue has not set, sealing the wood will probably prevent its doing so, and the first time you sit on the chair, you'll find the floor.

■ Before applying glue and clamping the pieces together, dry-fit them and ensure that the fit is good. Make any adjustments before applying glue and clamping the pieces together.

■ You will save yourself time and effort if you readjust the clamps so that only a turn or two is required to tighten them once they're in position.

6

7

8

9

10

home

There's an old English saying, 'A man's home is his castle', and let's face it, whether we live in a maisonette or a mansion, we all want it to be in good repair. We also want to make the most of it – from making a small lounge cosier, to fixing that damage in the carpet so well that you can't see the repair.

So that's what this section sets out to show you. We have design ideas on the main components of any home – the lounge, dining room, bedroom, bathroom and kitchen, plus some handy hints on keeping your home, your possessions and your family safer.

Remember that security is a 24-hour concern, and you can reinforce the effectiveness of a good alarm system with some simple measures that make entry even more difficult.

Previous page: *Use methylated spirits to keep all your chrome taps – and other chromed bathroom hardware – shiny and sparkling (see p. 96). The bewildering array of sanitary ware, fittings and accessories available allows you to create a bathroom perfectly suited to your needs and taste (see p. 92).*
This page: *A door that sticks is a nuisance – but luckily there is a simple solution to the problem (see p. 91).*

CARPETS

A CHILLING SOLUTION
Getting chewing gum off a carpet is eased when it is hardened, so freeze it with a few ice cubes in a plastic bag. Leave the bag on the gum for a few minutes and then use a blunt knife to pick it off. If it starts to soften again, reapply the ice pack for a while.

GET RID OF THAT CARPET STAIN
The first step is to get rid of the cause, so mop up the spilt liquid, using a dabbing action. Wiping it up will only drive it into the carpet. Then, treat as follows:

- Urine, excrement or vomit? Remove the solid material and dab the affected area with a solution of half a teaspoon of liquid detergent in half a litre of water. Follow this up by blotting the affected area with a solution of a tablespoon of ammonia to a cup of water. If the stain is still visible, apply a 50/50 solution of white vinegar and water – but test this first on a piece of carpet scrap or in an area in which any spot won't show, as white vinegar can remove some dyes. Finally, dab the area with a cloth dipped in clean water and allow to dry – dab with a dry cloth to speed up drying.
- Most water-soluble stains, such as a child's cool drink, can be removed simply with a mild detergent solution as above, followed by dabbing the area with a cloth dipped in clean water. When removing a stain, work from the outer edges inwards. The solution causing the stain is most concentrated at the centre, and if you work outwards from there, you tend to push the solution further.
- Remove grease stains by dabbing the stain with a nonflammable dry-cleaning agent, which you should first test on a carpet scrap or on a small hidden area of the carpet. Allow it to dry to confirm it will not affect the dye, before continuing. As above, dab, don't wipe, and work from the outer edges of the stain inwards.
- If the grease deposit is quite heavy, pouring hot water on it and then using a wet-dry vacuum to remove the same, will help get rid of most of the grease. The hot water melts it and it can then be sucked up. Repeat the procedure a couple of times until the deposit has been removed, then treat the stain as above.

FOREVER EMBER
A fire in winter is a delight – until an ember pops out and onto the carpet. Suddenly the laid-back, lethargic ambience of the evening is transformed into a mad scramble for tongs to grab the ember before it burns the carpet. Too late!

A solution is to cut a large piece of carpet offcut to fit across the floor in front of the fireplace. The ember may burn the offcut – but not the wall-to-wall. Just bear in mind that those embers may fly up to a metre or two, so be generous with the offcut. Roll it up and store it during the warmer months.

HINT
Use a fire screen as a precaution to prevent embers from the fire burning holes in carpets and upholstery.

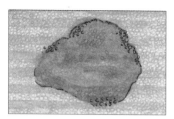

Oh, no!

Carefully remove the damaged section. Take care not to cut the underfelt.

Dry-fit the patch and trim if necessary.

Apply glue under the surrounding carpet and to the underside of the patch, and press in position.

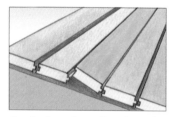

Replacing those floorboards is simple – even to the last, if you remove the lower lip.

PATCH IT

It is always a good idea to hang onto a few carpet scraps and offcuts when you have new wall-to-wall carpets installed – you never know when you may wish to test a cleaning solution on it, or need to patch it.

To apply a patch, do this:

1. Cut a rectangle or square out of the carpet just large enough to remove the damaged area. Make sure you cut along the weave and between the fibres on the crosscuts. Do not cut through the underfelt when removing the damaged area.
2. If your carpet has a pattern you will need to select a corresponding part of the offcut so that the pattern matches.
3. Cut your patch a couple of millimetres larger on each edge than the space it is to take, to ensure a seamless join.
4. Dry-fit the patch and trim if necessary. If you made it too short on any dimension, cut a new patch.
5. Once satisfied with the fit, lift the carpet from the underfelt and apply contact adhesive in a band about 50 mm wide around the patch, and then to the patch area itself and the underside of the patch.
6. Allow it to dry according to the maker's instructions, then press the carpet down onto the underfelt. Now, carefully – you have only one chance to get it right – push the patch into position, the edges first, and finally the centre. If you got it right, the patch will be virtually invisible and firmly in position, as the underfelt provides the link between the patch and the rest of the carpet.

FLOORS

REPLACE THOSE FLOORBOARDS
Floorboards are usually of the tongue-and-groove type, and this doesn't present a problem when you replace a number of them – until you reach the last one, that is. The lower lip will prevent the board slotting into place. So, remove it. Now the board will drop into position and you just need to secure it. If possible, attach it from below.

STOP THAT CREAKING
Creaking floorboards are often a fact of life when you live in a double-storey, timber-frame home, or one with a suspended wood floor. The creaking comes from wood moving against wood when a weight is applied – like a foot with a person's full weight on it, for instance.

First, locate the area of the creak – have someone walk about while you listen. Once you have located it, try one of these remedies:

- If the problem is one of a board moving against a joist, try tapping a small wedge into the gap between the underside of the board and the top of the joist.
- If it is one board moving against another, try lubricating the surfaces that are touching. Talcum powder, furniture wax, liquid soap and even ground-up pencil lead can work. You can also apply linseed oil to the boards – it will cause the wood to expand. As the flooring is tightened, movement may cease.

DOORS

LET'S GET THIS STRAIGHT!
- Aligning a cupboard door with its companion is a piece of cake when adjustable spring hinges are installed. The adjustment screws can be used to realign the door's swing in a few minutes. Loosen the screw holding the unit on its base plate. Then, making small adjustments and checking after each one, align the doors. Once they are aligned, tighten the locking screw on each hinge.
- When fitting ordinary butt hinges on a door, carefully align the door with its companion and mark the hinge positions lightly on the frame. Now use one of the hinges to mark the positions for the screws. Use just one screw per hinge to check that the door is aligned and, once satisfied, drive in the rest of the screws to attach the hinges firmly in position.

STICKING DOOR? SIMPLE SOLUTION
- If the bottom of the door catches on the outer end of its swing, a strip of card under one flap of the hinge will raise the bottom of the door. This will increase the gap between it and the floor, though you might have to sand the outer edge of the door if it catches on the jamb.
- To find out where a door might be catching, hold a piece of carbon paper, carbon side to the door, over the door where you think the problem might be. When you close it, problem areas will show up where the carbon is rubbed off. Sand down as necessary.

NO MORE SQUEAKS, NO MORE MESS
Stop excess oil dripping on your carpet by following these steps:

1. Tie a piece of string over the top hinge, pass it once around the lower hinge and allow the end to lie in the cap of a jar.
2. Apply oil to the top hinge. The excess oil will seep down the string and oil the lower hinge (though you can apply oil to that as well). And, finally, the end of the string will take all the excess oil into the receptacle. No squeaks, no mess.

The hinge base. The left-hand screw adjusts the angle of the hinge arm; the right-hand one locks it.

Turning the left-hand screw out moves the lower edge of the door out and up.

The locking screw allows the hinge arm to be moved in and out and when tightened, locks the hinge assembly in position.

The bathroom, usually the smallest room in the home, often allows as much creativity as any other area of the home as there is a bewildering array of sanitary ware, fittings and accessories available. It is also an area of the home in which old and new can be combined. It has to be practical, but it can also be modelled in a way that invites one to relax in the bath or jacuzzi, for instance.

- The first point is: don't skimp on the fittings and sanitary ware. The bathroom usually has a high humidity, and individual accessories get a hammering from steam. They are also subjected to stresses, such as when you use a handle to raise yourself from the bath.
- Secondly, most surfaces are dangerous when wet. So a nonslip floor material and a nonslip surface in the floor of the shower are important.
- The bath is a major component in a full bathroom, at least, so take care with the choice. Materials vary – from traditional cast iron, to acrylic, to pressed steel. Of the three, acrylic retains heat best, so your bath water stays hot longer. Baths range in size from 1,6 m to 1,8 m long. Triangular baths for corners are also available.
- Choose a design that makes things as easy as possible for you – like wall-mounted taps that are easy to reach from a reclining position.
- If you elect to have the spout at the end of the bath, make sure the plug fits well, or that the spout is not directly over the drain. It's not pleasant anticipating a long, luxurious soak, and returning to the bath to discover that the hot water has all gone down that drain because the plug was forced out and you are faced with a five-minute lick and a promise in tepid water!
- Handles on the side of the bath are a good idea; they make the bath more accessible and easier to use for older folk – and for you when you're older!
- Where possible, even if a shower is not part of the original bathroom, consider having a shower attachment installed over the bath, with a shower curtain to prevent splashing. Showers are more hygienic than baths and use much less water, thus saving on your electricity bills as well (less water for the geyser to reheat).
- Toilets are available in a wide variety of designs, colours and sizes. In this country, where water is often at a premium and water rationing is relatively common, it is a good idea to ensure that the cistern system you select has a flushing system that allows for a partial flush. You will save a lot of water.
- Basins, available in vitreous china, acrylic, fibreglass and porcelain, are also available in a variety of shapes and sizes.
- Bathroom heaters and heated towel rails might seem like a luxury, but on a cold winter's morning they turn an obligation into a pleasure.
- Mirrors not only help to make a bathroom seem larger; they also make it brighter.
- A light mounted over a mirror helps when a lady is applying make-up.
- Consider your colour scheme: shades of blue and green fit the water theme and enhance the overall effect. Contrast the dominant paint scheme with brightly coloured towels and pot plants – many varieties of plants thrive in bathrooms.
- Ventilation of the bathroom is important, one reason being to ensure the moisture-laden atmosphere after a bath is cleared relatively soon to reduce the incidence of mildew.

The ideal room for a mix of the old and the new. Here earthy colours and a variety of textures are combined with simple chrome fittings.

Painting the door while it's level like this not only saves you having to bend, but also ensures that the paint won't run.

PAINTING DOORS THE EASY WAY

Instead of having to crawl about on hands and knees when painting a bedroom door, do it the easy way!

1. Tap the hinge pins out (bottom hinge first!) and drive two nails into the top and base, making sure that they're stout nails and driven in at least 25 mm or so. Drive in more if you're in any doubt.
2. Rest the door on the nail ends and paint one side. Allow the paint to dry.
3. Flip the door over and paint the other side.
4. Once the job is complete, remove the nails and rehang the door.

A BIT WARPED?

When a cupboard door is a bit warped, put it into a reverse warp.

1. Put a block of wood under the inwardly bowed side and use a sash clamp to pull the outwardly bowed end into the frame.
2. Leave it like this for a week and then repeat the treatment if necessary.

WINDOWS

REPLACING A BROKEN WINDOW SAFELY

Wear thick gloves, such as those welders use, to avoid cutting yourself, and also wear eye protection.

- Apply a number of strips of duct tape to a broken windowpane before you start removing the putty or beading. Once you are ready to remove the pane, it will come free largely in one piece – albeit a broken one.
- When removing broken shards of glass, pull rather than push – if it snaps, slivers of glass will break away on the far side of the glass, instead of towards you.
- Clean the rabbet (the notch the pane fits into) for the new pane, removing any old putty. Then give it a coat of linseed oil to stop it absorbing the oil in the putty.
- Lay tape around the rim of the new pane, a suitable distance from the edge. When you apply the putty, you simply have to remove the tape afterwards for a neat edge.
- When the window's frame is wood, the pane will be held in place with battens – and driving in the panel pins could see you cracking the new pane. So, just hold a sheet of plywood against the pane to protect it, and tap the panel pins into the frame.

SEALING A LEAKING WINDOW

Run foam rubber sealing tape with a self-adhesive backing around the inner edge of the window at the top and sides – not the bottom. The foam rubber will compress, forming a tight weatherproof fit, and any water that does penetrate will be able to escape through the unsealed bottom edge.

SHELVES

ANCHORS FOR ATTACHING ITEMS TO DRY WALLS

There is a variety of fasteners available for this purpose but, where possible, you should attach the shelf to a dry wall by driving the screw through the wallboard and directly into a wall stud. If that is not possible, however, you will have to use one of the following:

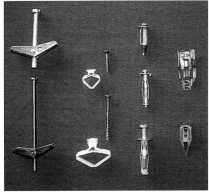

Wherever possible, when attaching items to a dry wall, try to drive the screws into the wall studs for a stronger support. Wallboard and wallboard anchors will support only light to moderate loads.

- Toggle bolt – will take a moderate load on a dry wall. Drill a hole large enough for the bolt's wings when they are folded back, and ensure you put washers and any bracket on the bolt **before** you push the wings into its hole. Close the wings, push them into the hole so that they can spring open on the other side.
- Plastic toggle – suitable for a moderate load on wallboard. Drill a hole the same diameter as the anchor, close the plastic wings and tap the anchor into its hole. Slip a bracket or washer onto the screw and drive it home. It will lock onto the wings on the far side, pulling them up hard against the wallboard's inner surface.
- Hollow-wall anchor (also known as a Molly bolt) – suitable for moderate loads on wallboard, and for attaching clothes hooks to hollow-core doors, for instance. Drill a hole of the same diameter as the anchor and seat it in the hole. Tighten the bolt to pull the wings hard up against the inner surface, then remove the bolt and attach the bracket to the dry wall.
- Metal drive-in anchor – moderate load on wallboard. Drill a 3-mm starter hole and then hammer the anchor into the wallboard. Then slip the bracket over the screw and attach to the wall.

NOTE: All these anchors for use in wallboards are suitable for light to moderate loads only.

ANCHORS FOR ATTACHING ITEMS TO MASONRY WALLS

Anchors for use on masonry walls will generally take heavier loads than any load on a dry wall or hollow-core door.

- Plastic wall anchor – the smaller they are, the lighter the loads they are able to bear, but they are available in a wide range of sizes and the biggest ones can support a substantial load. Drill a hole slightly smaller than the diameter of the anchor and tap it into its hole, slip the item over the screw and drive it home.

HINT

Behind every dry wall is a framework of studs (vertical beams) to which the panels are attached. Electronic 'stud-finders' are available, but failing that, tap along the panel until the sound changes from 'hollow' to 'solid', or where you can see the panel has been attached to the stud, and drive your screws in there. Attaching items such as shelving directly to the studs achieves a far stronger attachment.

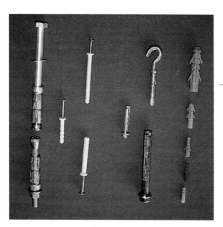

Depending on the type of anchor used, you can support very heavy loads on masonry walls.

HINT

One day you may have to move an item you have attached to a masonry wall, but the holes for the attachment bolts – and perhaps the bolts themselves – remain, and they do not look good! Removing a projecting bolt anchor, is difficult if not impossible – so why bother? Cut the end of the bolt off as close as you can to the wall's surface, and use the offcut, held in a pair of pliers, and a club hammer to drive the remaining piece into the wall. Fill, sand and repaint as necessary.

- Metal sleeve anchor – suitable for heavy loads. Drill a hole of the same diameter as the sleeve and insert it into the hole. As the nut is tightened, the tapered end of the bolt spreads the sleeve, which in turn locks tightly in the hole.
- Nail anchor (not pictured) – comprises an alloy sleeve into which its nail is driven. Drill a hole of the same diameter as the sleeve and tap it in position. Slip the item to be attached on the nail, and drive it into the sleeve.
- Frame-fixing anchor – comprises a plastic sleeve into which a fastener can be driven with a hammer or screwdriver.
- Segmented metal shield anchor – suitable for the heaviest loads, this anchor consists of a segmented metal shield surrounding a tapered insert. Drill a hole of the same diameter as the shield and tap it into the hole. As the bolt is tightened, the tapered section is drawn forward, locking the shield segments hard against the sides of the hole.
- Projecting bolt anchor – suitable for very heavy loads and works on the same principle as the abovementioned anchor. Here, however, the threaded rod replaces the bolt. As the nut is tightened, it pulls the bolt forward, pulling the tapered end into the shield and locking it against the sides of the hole. The nut can then be removed and the item slipped onto the protruding section of the bolt.

Deeper is cheaper

The deeper the anchor is, the stronger the attachment, so make sure you drill the hole well below the plaster and into the masonry itself. If you do not go deep enough, you may find that you do not have a strong enough attachment, and you'll need to buy another bolt because you cannot get the first one out.

Brinkmanship!

Beware of inserting shield bolts too close to the end of a wall or column. They exert tremendous force on the surrounding masonry and will cause fractures if placed too close to an unsupported edge.

THAT'S THE SPIRIT!

There's more to methylated spirits than colour. Apart from its use as a fuel, methylated spirits is also useful in the following cases:

- Getting rid of aphids on house plant leaves: dab the leaves with a ball of cotton wool soaked in methylated spirits. **Don't use this trick on plants with sensitive leaves, such as African violets.**
- Don't want that old bumper sticker to disfigure your car any more? Simply scrape off as much as you can and then use methylated spirits to soften any glue deposits.
- Got a carpenter bee problem in your woodwork? Use a syringe to inject some methylated spirits into the holes made by the bees.
- Put the shine back in your life – methylated spirits is very effective for shining chrome taps and other bathroom hardware.

FURNITURE

REUPHOLSTERING A CHAIR

Re-covering the seat on a dining-room chair, for instance, is not difficult.

For the sake of simplicity, we have assumed in this case that the seat foam is in good repair. You can elect to remove the existing covering fabric, or leave it in place if it is simply a case of covering for a new effect. If the existing covering is ripped, then it is best to remove it.

You will need a piece of the new covering fabric large enough to overlap the frame of the seat, on all sides, by about 100 mm.

1. Remove the seat from the chair and remove the existing covering (if necessary) and undercover material. Lay the piece of new covering fabric face down on a firm surface and place the seat, upside down, in the centre.
2. Aligning the seat carefully, staple the new cover to the under-side of the seat's frame at the front (fold the edge of the fabric under, so that the staples pass through two layers of fabric). You will find it easier to attach the parallel edges of the chair first – in this case, the front and rear.
3. Working from the rear side of the seat, pull the fabric tight so that it fits snugly over the foam, and staple as you did with the front. It is best to staple in the centre first, then near each corner, and then to fill the spaces between the three with staples at intervals of about 30 mm. Leave the extreme corners unstapled for the moment.
4. Now follow the same procedure with the two sides. Check to ensure that you are not pulling too hard, otherwise you will distort any pattern on the fabric.
5. You are now left with four corners. At each one in turn, pull the fabric up so that it fits snugly, hold it as shown, and staple on either side of the 'sail' you are holding between your fingers. To finish the corner, fold the 'sail' into an arrowhead shape, flat against the underside of the frame, and staple securely into position.
6. To complete the job, staple the undercover material in posi-tion to ensure a neat finish to the job, and reattach the seat to the chair.

Fold under and staple the front edge first.

Next, pull the fabric tight, taking care not to distort it, and staple the rear edge.

Trim off excess fabric and attach each side, leaving the corners to last. Hold the corner 'sail' up and staple along the base on each side.

Trim excess material from each corner, fold the end under and staple. Complete the job by attaching the cover and reattach the seat to the chair.

THE KITCHEN

Never underestimate the value of a well-fitted kitchen – more than once it has been the deciding factor when a potential buyer has viewed a home for sale. Furthermore, the kitchen is not just a place for preparing food. It is also a social centre in the home and the place where mom and just about everyone else spend a lot of time.

- So you're looking for something that is practical, attractive, easy to maintain and designed around the work triangle – the stove, refrigerator and sink – with plenty of work surface between. The three units need to make a triangle with good separation between all three and positioned so that a person working at one will not be in the way of someone working at another – accidents happen when people collide and they're carrying hot pots!
- The kitchen is the site for a dishwasher, microwave oven and possibly a washing machine and tumble dryer as well, and these need to be situated where they do not interfere with the main traffic between the 'big three'. Obviously, they are important. The dishwasher can be placed near the sink so that larger scraps of food can be rinsed off plates and dishes before they go into the washer, and the microwave oven needs to be where it is conveniently accessible from where the food is prepared. The washing machine and tumble dryer, however, can be a little more 'out of the way' since it is unlikely that they will be used, loaded or unloaded while a meal is being prepared.
- Easy-to-clean and durable work surfaces, and a surface with the same qualities behind the stove, are essential. There is a wide variety on the market – from laminates, such as Formica, to tiles, granite, marble, wood and stainless steel. Each one has its merits and drawbacks. For instance, laminates are available in a variety of colours, as are tiles, granite and marble to some extent. Most surfaces are heat-resistant to a greater or lesser extent, but there are a number of other factors to consider.
- A tiled surface is very resistant to heat, but can crack if a kitchen utensil or pot is dropped on it. Replacing a tile is not difficult, however – just remember to store quite a few extra of every type when having a tiled surface installed. A drawback to a tiled surface is the accumulation of food particles in the grouting between the tiles, so thorough cleaning is a must.
- A laminated surface is less heat-resistant, and the entire surface has to be replaced if part of it is burned.
- Marble and granite are heat-resistant and very hard-wearing, but also expensive. Artificial versions are available, however.
- Wood is an excellent surface if you want to create a 'cottagey' effect, but ensure it is well sealed to avoid staining. Heat resistance is a problem as well.
- The colour scheme should be light and bright – the more garish the colours, the weirder food might look. Cool colours, like green, blue, creams and natural colours such as wood-textured cupboard doors will create the impression you're seeking.
- Food preparation requires good lighting, and fittings to direct light onto the top of the stove and work surfaces are a good idea. The average kitchen, with its eye-level cupboards, provides ample scope for lighting. Downlighters, mounted in the bases of the top cupboards, are ideal for lighting work surfaces.

- Having sufficient storage space in a kitchen is also essential. In fact, make that 'more than sufficient'. But with such scope for cupboards in a kitchen, one can create a huge amount of storage space. Work surfaces should be at a height of about 900 mm, with cupboards above them starting at 1,45 m. If necessary, use drop-in shelves (see page 39) to increase the storage space, and use a lazy Susan in a corner which would otherwise be a difficult place to reach stored items. Group taller cupboards, rather than placing them individually.

- As delicious as the meal may be, having the smell of cooking wafting through the home and during dinner can be a little off-putting. Hence, ventilation – either through natural means such as an adequate window area, or a combination of this and a cooker hood and extractor fan – is a must.

- The floor should comprise a hard-wearing, durable and nonslip surface, and a good choice for a kitchen might be studded rubber matting. It is easily cleaned and nonslip, and you're less likely to break a bowl or cup on it. Other kitchen flooring you might consider are ceramic tiles, quarry tiles, vinyl and linoleum.

Downlighters, either mounted in the base of a cupboard or hidden in a recess, are an absolute must – especially when the work surface is made of a dark-coloured material.

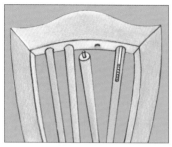

Accurate drilling, glue, a piece of dowel and a spring for a hidden repair.

Labels make reassembly easy.

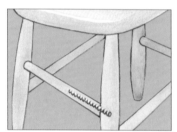

Glue grips a threaded rod insert, making an effective repair.

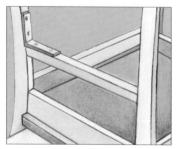

A small metal bracket is an effective reinforcement for a joint. Not for use on your antiques!

SOME SIMPLE CHAIR REPAIRS

Spring into action – repair that spindle

A broken rung in a chair back can be replaced – but usually only if you take the back apart. However, it can be repaired and replaced without disassembling the back by following this procedure:

1. Remove the broken spindle and accurately drill a hole down each shaft – obviously, you must ensure that the holes will correspond exactly when the broken halves are placed together.
2. Cut a length of threaded rod of the same diameter as the holes, but a few millimetres shorter than their combined depth. Apply glue to the holes and broken surfaces and reassemble the spindle. The threads on the rod give the glue a surface to grip.
3. Once the repair is complete, drill another hole into the top of the spindle and a corresponding one into the chair back where the spindle meets it. Trim the spindle sufficiently so that the end will be able to fit in snugly under the back, and slip the end you cut off into its hole in the back.
4. Now insert a spring into the hole in the spindle and place a dowel on top. The top end of the latter must be flush with the top of the spindle when the spring is fully compressed.
5. Apply glue to the bottom end of the spindle, to the dowel and to the dowel's hole in the chair back. Insert the lower end of the spindle into its socket, depress the dowel and push the top of the spindle into position. As the two holes line up, the spring pushes the dowel into its hole in the chair back and the spindle is fixed in position.

Taking a chair apart?

Use hot vinegar to remove old glue. It softens it so that you can scrape it out of the joints. And vinegar won't harm the finish.

Keeping tabs

Before taking a chair or piece of furniture apart, make up little labels from masking tape and mark both component parts of each joint – A-A, B-B and so on. It will make matching up the parts a piece of cake.

A rod works well

A threaded rod can be used to repair a broken chair joint. The glue will grip the thread quite effectively, but use a small bracket if necessary to reinforce the joint even further.

You can't beat a bracket

Joints can fail quickly when they pull apart, but they stay sound while the components are properly seated – and a small metal bracket will help do that. It is quite an obvious repair, however, and therefore not suitable for your more valuable items.

Buckle down for a temporary repair

If the joints on a chair or set of kitchen steps work loose, a length of wire and a turnbuckle will keep the unit together until you can carry out a permanent repair.

1. Unscrew the turnbuckle as far as possible and attach one end of the wire to one end.
2. Holding the turnbuckle midway between the chair or steps' legs, pass the wire around the legs, pull it reasonably tight, and attach the end to the other end of the turnbuckle.
3. Place a cushion of stout cardboard under the wire where it meets the legs, and tighten the turnbuckle sufficiently to hold the chair or steps' legs firmly in position.

A close shave

When the end of a spindle is too small for its socket, glue a piece of wood shaving of even thickness around the end of the spindle before you glue it into its socket.

It's just a veneer

When a mortise-and-tenon joint, for instance, has worked loose, or you cut the tenon too small when making up a replacement part, try glueing strips of veneer to the sides.

SOME SIMPLE DRAWER TRICKS

Just stop it!

Many of us have pulled a drawer out too far and had the contents all over the floor. A simple stop at the back of the drawer will prevent this. Drill a hole through a piece of wood long enough to hang vertically on the back of the drawer, with its top protruding above the back of the drawer. It will stop the drawer being removed accidentally. To remove the drawer intentionally, simply swing the stop to a horizontal position and the drawer can be removed.

Sticking?

When a drawer sticks, often a little lubrication is enough to solve the problem – talcum powder or furniture wax being good choices. If that doesn't solve the problem, try tapping a drawing pin into the front of the frame where the drawer's sides ride on it. The head of the pin provides a smooth surface on which the edges can move.

Anchor that knob

Drawer knobs sometimes work loose through constant use. The trick is to drill a 1-mm or 2-mm hole about 5 mm into the base of the knob, and a corresponding hole into the front of the drawer next to the knob attachment point. Cut a panel pin or thin nail to length and insert it into the hole in the knob. Align it with the corresponding hole and fix the knob in position with the attachment screw. Now the knob cannot turn and will remain firmly attached to the drawer front.

A turnbuckle and wire will keep that frame in one piece until you can make a permanent repair.

This swinging arm stops the drawer being pulled out too far.

A small nail stops the knob working loose.

REMOVING STAINS FROM WOOD

GET RID OF THAT GLASS RING
The white ring a cup or glass leaves is one of the most common stains on furniture. You can try cigarette or cigar ash in a little cooking oil. Rub the stain with the tip of your finger moistened with the solution. If the stain still remains, try table salt and a little water, mayonnaise or toothpaste. If you still have not had success, silver polish or car polish might work. If none of these work, the only real alternative is to refinish the surface entirely.

GET RID OF THAT INK STAIN
Raw linseed oil and fine steel wool can be effective in removing ink stains. Ensure that you use minimal pressure when doing this, to avoid scarring the surface.

CAUTION
This sort of remedy can be applied to most surfaces, but if the furniture that has been stained is really valuable, or an antique, have the stain removed professionally.

GUIDELINES FOR REMOVING STAINS
- Where possible, once you have removed the worst of a deposit from a fabric, turn it over and spray it hard from the other side. This will force the offending substance out, whereas spraying from the upper side, on which the substance landed, will tend to push particles further into the fabric.
- Be careful when you are using bleach – check that you won't do more damage to the fabric.
- Lastly, the sooner you get going on the stain, the better.

REMOVING STAINS FROM FABRICS

GET RID OF THAT STAIN
A bewildering variety of substances and fluids can stain fabrics – including carpets, clothing and furniture. Here are a few of the more common problems, and how to get rid of them (also see page 89):

- **Blood:** The sooner you get it off the better, so the first step is to wash the blood out in cool water. If the blood has dried, dab it with meat tenderiser and add cool water. It will take about 20 minutes or so to soften the stain, after which you should sponge it off with cool water. And blood on leather can be removed with a little hydrogen peroxide dabbed onto the deposit, wiping it off after the bubbling has commenced.
- **Chocolate:** Remove the worst of the deposit, then a solution of half a teaspoon of mild detergent in 500 ml water dabbed on the stain with a clean cloth should do the trick. If not, try a solution of a tablespoon of ammonia in half a cup of water, and dab as before.
- **Coffee:** Sponge with a solution of borax. If the stain still remains, beat an egg yolk and rub it into the stain with a clean white cloth,

then rinse in clean water. You can also spray with a branded stain remover and then rinse in clean water.

- **Grass:** Try rubbing the stain with a pad dipped in liquid detergent or a diluted solution of alcohol. White vinegar, a mild solution of hydrogen peroxide, or bleach – if safe for the fabric – can be tried on very stubborn stains.
- **Ink (ballpoint):** Sponge with methylated spirits or mineral turpentine, then rub with a detergent solution. You can also try hair spray or nail polish remover, but first test this on a part of the fabric that is hidden.
- **Ink (felt-tip):** Sponge with methylated spirits or gently rub liquid detergent into the stain and then rinse off in clean water. Dabbing the stain with dry-cleaning solvent or bleach (if safe for the fabric) is another alternative.
- **Lipstick:** Treat the stain with methylated spirits or salad oil, or rub in petroleum jelly, cold cream or white margarine and wipe with white bread. Soak the stain in lemon juice if the garment is white, and in a 50/50 water/juice solution if it is coloured.
- **Rust:** Rub a vinegar/salt paste into the stain, leave to stand for 30 minutes and wash.

BRASS

DON'T GET BRASSED OFF
Brass is great in the home – until it has to be cleaned and polished. But here's an easy way:

1. Simply soak each piece in a solution of one dessertspoon of tartaric acid and half a dessertspoon of liquid dishwasher in a sinkful of warm water.
2. Wash the brass item, rinse off in clean cold water and dry with a soft cloth. The shine should last about a month.

NOTE: With bigger items, such as a brass kist, or a handle, apply the same solution with a soft brush, rinse off with clean water and dry.

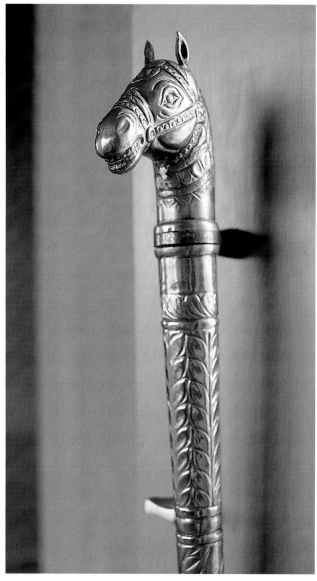

Brass can be a beautiful feature in the home, but only while the shine lasts. Follow the two easy steps (above) for a longer-lasting shine!

THE LOUNGE

The lounge is the room where the family gets together at times other than mealtimes, and it is the room used to entertain visitors. So it is very much a family and people room, and their needs will dictate how the room is arranged.

Fortunately, it is usually one of the largest rooms in the home and so, though considered one of the more important ones, you generally have a little more latitude in how the furniture and other items are arranged. It is also, in many if not most homes, the entertainment room – with the TV taking a prominent role in how the furniture is arranged. If this is the case in your home, you might like to take advantage of a long lounge to create two distinct areas – one for viewing the TV or listening to music, the other for conversation.

■ A fireplace is a natural focal point and the conversation area will be created to best effect around it.

■ The lounge's shape will have a major influence on how you arrange the furniture, which needs to be positioned to create a conversation area. If the lounge is rectangular and long enough, you might have more options than if it is square.

■ You can also use various furnishings and effects to create a different 'look'. For instance, when its shape is square, selecting items of furniture that are low will help create an impression of length. If the walls are papered, then a design with a horizontal theme will enhance the effect. In contrast, a lounge that is very definitely rectangular can be made to seem shorter by selecting furniture that is higher, and adding a vertical aspect to the walls, for example by hanging ceiling-to-floor curtains – their vertical folds help 'shorten' the length of the lounge – which will also make the room cosier.

■ The colour scheme is all-important, obviously, and needs a lot of thought. If you have a young family, and your lounge is to have wall-to-wall carpeting, one of your priorities might be being able to hide the damage; in this case a carpet with a mottled, irregular pattern can be a good choice. Generally, lighter colours on walls and of carpets and curtains will make the room seem larger, while darker hues will have the opposite effect. Warm colours – yellow or orange – tend to do exactly that . . . warm the lounge, while cool colours – light pastels, for instance – do the opposite. A major point with colour selection is this: a colour swatch might look great in your hand or held against the wall. But paint the whole wall that colour and you could be shocked at the result. Another point to bear in mind is that colour takes on different hues in different light, as the sun passes overhead during the day and then as the lights go on at night. So check that colour swatch a few times during the day, and in the evening, before deciding.

■ Allied to that, the way you light your lounge can help make or break the effect you are trying to create. If your lounge will be used for reading, you will need good light in that part of the room. Bouncing light off the ceiling or light-coloured walls will help create a cosy, subdued atmosphere. And if you have a favourite picture, highlighting it will create another focal point for the room.

■ A contrast of patterns versus plain is also worth considering, as furniture with a patterned fabric might clash with a boldly patterned carpet, and the whole effect might not be what you wanted. Using single-colour carpeting or tiles in conjunction with furniture with a patterned fabric is more likely to create a good effect than patterned in both cases, or plain in both. On the other hand, either combination might work brilliantly!

■ The bottom line: At the end of the day, your décor is yours. Whether you go for a modern, angular style, traditional, country, Mediterranean or eclectic – in which you draw from a variety of styles to create your own very special effect – it is a result with which you need to be happy.

■ For ideas, study décor magazines and books, and visit home-decorating exhibitions. And chat to the experts there. Then go home and create something amazing.

Use low-slung furniture to create an intimate conversation area in a big open-plan space.

HINT

It's a match! A simple and effective counter to unpleasant odours is . . . light a match. Not quite perfume, but it's better than the alternative. An aromatic candle is also a useful aid in countering those odours that make your eyes water.

VINYL

CLEAN THAT VINYL SURFACE THE GENTLE WAY

Don't use harsh means to clean vinyl; you're likely to damage it. You should be able to clean vinyl of most grime using the following method:

1. Make up a solution of a quarter cup each of bicarbonate of soda and washing powder in two cups of warm water. Ensure that the ingredients dissolve totally.
2. Moisten kitchen paper or a rough-textured cloth with the solution and vigorously rub the vinyl surface.

ODOURS

DON'T LET THAT SMELL RUIN YOUR APPETITE

Prevention is better than cure, so pack food in freezers in purpose-made freezer bags.

But even then you can still end up with unpleasant odours emanating from your refrigerator or freezer. If that should happen, try these remedies:

- Put bicarbonate of soda on a number of small trays – make up a few out of aluminium foil – and leave them in the freezer or refrigerator for a while.
- Wash the appliance's interior surfaces with a bicarbonate of soda solution once a month.
- When defrosting the appliance, use a warm solution of bicarbonate of soda to clean the surfaces.

BIN THERE, DONE THAT

When your rubbish bin begins to smell, sprinkle some cat litter in the bottom of the bin. Renew the litter when the bottom of the bin gets damp.

TRUNK CALL

A trunk that has been unused for some time will often get a musty smell – and cat litter works well here too. Make up a foil tray as in the case of the freezer problem, fill it with the litter material, place it in the bottom of the trunk and close the lid – within a day or so the musty odour will have disappeared.

GIVE A ROOM A NEW ATMOSPHERE

Spray some cologne onto a cool light bulb – note, it must be cool (if you spray a hot bulb, it will shatter). When you turn the light on, the heat of the bulb causes the aroma to be wafted through the room.

HINT

Bar heaters and fires tend to dry out the air in a room. Place a bowl of water near the heat source to 'humidify' the room, and add a little deodorant to it to perfume the air at the same time.

PLANT THIS IDEA IN YOUR MIND

Planting aromatic plants on the windward side of your home near a window will ensure that the plant's scent will pervade the house.

ROOFS

GET THAT GUTTER CLEAN

Why clamber up and down a ladder to clean gutters? A hose tied to a clamp on the end of a length of timber will allow you to walk along, washing the gutter as you go. All that's required would be a quick check later to ensure that you haven't missed any spots.

MAKE A MESH OF IT

Leaves are a curse when they fall into gutters and cause rainwater to dam up. They're even more of a problem if they block a downpipe. So, the best is to stop them falling into the gutter in the first place. There are purpose-made mesh panels that fit into gutters, but you can also make them up from the plastic mesh designed for plant trellises or, at a push, make them out of chicken mesh.

KEEP THE MOSS AWAY

Moss and fungus do not like copper, so if you are troubled with growths of these on your roof, fix a few lengths of bare copper wire along the peak of your roof, or on both sides, just below it.

SOME SIMPLE REPAIRS

Modern single-lap roof tiles are strong, but they can be broken – however, replacing them is not difficult:

1. Use small wedges to lift the lower end of the left-hand tile over-lapping the broken one and the one directly above it.
2. You should now be able to lift the broken tile out, levering up-wards if it is held in place with a clip.
3. Slide the replacement tile into place, remove the wedges and ease the surrounding tiles back into place.

NOTE: If you cannot obtain a replacement tile immediately, follow the removal procedure as above, and wrap a small sheet of plastic around the tile. Then put it back into position. It might not look very good, but will keep leaks at bay until you can make a proper repair.

A hose tied to a clamp on a length of wood makes a useful aid to cleaning gutters.

This way you can clean your gutter without having to shift a ladder along all the time. Simply check at the end of the task and sort out any problem areas.

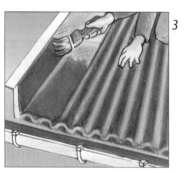

Fixing the flashing where a roof meets a wall is simple, and there are excellent products on the market to make it even easier.

The first step, once you're up on the roof, is to clean the area you will be repairing – and don't forget any of the safety tips we gave you at the beginning of this book. Use a wire brush to get rid of any loose debris and make sure you remove any of the old flashing that has deteriorated badly and is loose. You need to ensure that your new flashing will be bonded properly to the surface and any loose material will prevent this.

If necessary, once you have cleaned the surface to your satisfaction, hose it down or, by far the better alternative, use a blower to blast loose material away. The latter method is advisable for two reasons: spraying water over the surface will also mean some will get through the gaps and go down your walls and, secondly, the surface should be dry, so using water will entail a delay. So, beg, borrow or hire a blower if you can – it's the best choice.

Right, once you're satisfied you've prepared the surface, you're ready to begin:

1. Apply a thick coat of compound along the area to be repaired. The width of the coating should be slightly wider than that of the mesh you're laying down and you should make sure you get it into every nook and cranny.
2. Immediately after applying the coating, press the mesh into the wet compound (you'll need rubber gloves for this job!). Press the mesh down well to ensure that it conforms to the surface along its entire length and breadth – including all those nooks and crannies – and is properly bonded to the surface. Remember that any gap you leave could allow the ingress of water and moisture. The compound will be seen to seep through the mesh and should do so everywhere – where the mesh retains its original colour, you have a pocket of air, and no bond!
3. When the first bonding layer of compound is completely dry, apply a second coat, allow it to dry, and then follow up with two more, or one more plus your coat of exterior paint. **At each stage, be sure to allow sufficient time for the previous coat to dry properly.**

HINTS
■ You will find it best if you apply the coating in stages, say 600 mm long, then rolling out the mesh and pressing it in, and then doing the next 600 mm. It is essential that the compound is still wet and can permeate the mesh completely, and if you do the job on a hot day and coat the entire length

to be repaired, the coating could be too dry towards the end of laying the mesh.

■ If you are using two or more rolls of mesh, ensure you provide an overlap of, say, 50-100 mm where the new roll starts. Press the end of the old roll into the wet compound, then apply some compound to the last 50-100 mm of its upper surface, and press the first 50-100 mm of the new roll into the compound.

■ This sounds simple, but it's easier than you think to make a mistake: ensure that when overlapping the mesh, the mesh being laid further down the slope goes under the length above it, so that a watertight join is assured and rainwater flows off it.

IT'S A ROTTEN BUSINESS

The two types of rot you may find are dry rot and wet rot, and both are caused by fungi.

Dry rot

If an area is damp and unventilated, you have the perfect conditions for dry rot – a much more serious condition than wet rot. The condition resembles rust-coloured lichen in the shape of a pancake. The rim is white or light grey and getting rid of it is a job for the professionals. The entire infestation must be killed off or it can lie dormant for years and then re-establish itself.

The most common areas of infestation are under floors, behind skirting boards and under paint. The signs are dry, soft brittle wood that cracks easily across the grain. It has a musty smell.

When the repairs have been made, ensure that every scrap of infected wood is burned to kill off the spores.

Wet rot

If you find an area of wood that has become soft and pulpy, turns dark and shrinks, and cracks along the grain, suspect wet rot. Sparse white or dark strands might also be visible on its surface.

It occurs when wood becomes very wet, frequently, and does not get a chance to dry out completely.

The first step is to eliminate the cause of the damp and then to treat the wood with a preservative such as PCP.

GET RID OF MOULD

Mould takes root in warm, damp conditions and can effect grout, paint and wallpaper. Bleach should be considered a temporary cure as it does not kill the roots; for a more permanent solution, wash the surface with a warm solution of detergent and water or soap and water and then apply a fungicide according to the maker's instructions.

Where wallpaper has been so damaged that it has to be replaced, use an adhesive treated with a fungicide to apply the new paper.

HINT
Foliage obscures the sun, so if deep shade is contributing to wet rot, pruning back trees and shrubs will help the drying process. Be ruthless – it's cheaper in the long run.

The bedroom is the room in the home for its occupant, and it is the one room where they can allow their imagination to run riot. So there are few rules and, in any event, they will tend to change as a child grows from toddler and preteen to teenager, and finally (you hope) moves out to his or her own place! But there are a few ideas that one can consider:

- The bed in the bedroom is the focus. It's usually the largest item in the room and everything else has to be positioned accordingly. There is a wide variety of styles and materials from which to choose – from hard-wearing and economical pine for the kids to lush padded oak, brass or wrought iron for mom and dad.

- A prime position for the bed is not next to a window or where it will block the flow through the room. Placing it as close as possible to a power point eliminates the need for unsightly cords tacked along the skirting boards. You will also need to allow space for a bedside table or similar surface on which a bedside lamp can be placed, and to ensure that it does not prevent cupboard doors being opened fully. So, the bed comes first, and the other items of furniture are placed thereafter.

- As with many other aspects of the bedroom, the colour scheme should be an expression of the occupant's (or occupants') tastes, but as with any other room in the home, light colours create an impression of space, while darker hues make it seem smaller.

- Lighting will have an important impact on the overall effect. The bedside light should provide adequate light for reading in bed, and if there is a desk in the room, it too should have its own light. Incidentally, if possible, position a desk in front of the window for maximum light during the day. If the main light is a centre light hanging from the ceiling, it is worth considering having an opaque fitting that envelops the whole light. This will provide good lighting but avoid the garishness of a bare bulb – the impact of which can be great if it is switched on when the occupant is asleep.

- A corner double bunk bed with a small desk under the upper bunk gives a child space to do his homework undisturbed.

- Children tend to drop things (so do we, for that matter!) so you might consider laying carpet tiles rather than wall-to-wall carpets. At least, if there are spills and stains you cannot remove, you have to replace only the damaged tiles.

- Make those walls washable: there is a wide range of top-quality paints available that can be easily cleaned and this is a distinct advantage when you have a young child.

Combine earthy tones and a minimum of decorative items to create a tranquil, relaxed atmosphere in the bedroom.

TERMITES ARE BIG TROUBLE – BECOME A TERMITENATOR

Since termites can severely damage the woodwork of a house, their eradication is best left to the experts, but you can reduce the risk by keeping the area around the home and under it – if you have a timber house on columns – clear of rubbish. Keep an eye out for signs of termites and when you see any, don't waste time making the right moves.

BANISH BORERS

If you spot a small hole in a piece of timber, and possibly a deposit of fine wood particles surrounding it, suspect borers.

Brush PCP or an antiborer product over all the surfaces, paying special attention to any holes you find. You can also use a syringe with a blunted needle to inject the fluid into the holes.

SECURITY

SECURITY – KEEPING YOUR FAMILY, YOUR HOME AND YOURSELF SAFE

Security in and around the home is something in which the whole family should be involved. Naturally, one should not become paranoid, but there is no doubt that a family that is aware of even the most basic of security measures is less likely to suffer loss – whether human or material.

- A multilayered approach is best, and the first and probably most important aspect is awareness. Any security measure is only as good as the people using it. An alarm system is no good if it is allowed to fall into disrepair. Burglar bars are of absolutely no use if the front door is left open. A peephole is completely useless if the door is opened to all and sundry without any check to see who's out there.
- You should ensure that you test your alarm system at least once a month, and if it is connected to a control room, make sure that they are notified beforehand. Make a point of checking the panic buttons.
- Learn to think as a potential burglar or hijacker might think. This will help you close loopholes in your security system and in your level of awareness.
- Make sure the simple measures are in place – always! Keep keys in a recognised place. Keep portable alarm devices in the same place when they are not on your person.
- Be aware of what is going on around you and in your neighbourhood.

HINT

If you use ordinary screws to attach burglar bars to windows so that you can remove them periodically for painting, a blob of solder in each slot will prevent an intruder from unscrewing them from the outside.

- Often, the only thing between severe loss and the prevention of a crime is an alert neighbour. By the same token, more than once alert neighbours, while unable to prevent a crime being committed, have been instrumental in the swift apprehension of the perpetrators – which is likely to have prevented further crime.
- Finally, be aware of your rights. Remember that you might have only a second or two to decide what to do when faced with a threat. The courts have days and weeks – and you could end up in trouble for taking the wrong tack when defending what is yours.

Use gravel chips around the house as an added security measure, especially in areas hidden from view by high walls. Besides adding loads of atmosphere, gravel makes a silent approach almost impossible.

And the point of this is . . . what? He just hops over from next door.

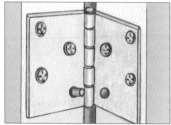

A protruding pin replacing one hinge screw provides extra safety.

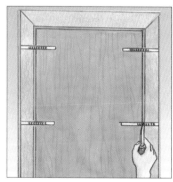

For a door you seldom use, or which to secure while on holiday, this is very effective.

KEEP YOUR PET SAFE

A trend has developed recently – poisoning the family's dog before breaking into the home. The antidote is to train your dog to take food only from its designated bowl, which is kept in just one area; at the back door, for instance. That will prevent outsiders poisoning your dog. This is probably a better course of training than teaching the dog to accept food only from certain people – if they are all absent for any reason, there could be a problem getting the dog to eat.

GET THE POINT?

It is amazing how many people put razor-sharp ridges along the top of whatever they have on their front boundary, but leave the tops of the support columns bare – for example where they are used to support wrought-iron work. People also tend to run the deterrent topping to the exact boundary of their property, and no further. So what's to stop an intruder climbing over the bare-topped support pillar, or simply going next door and hopping over the unprotected wall?

If you're going to protect your property's boundary, do the whole thing – you may even be able to get your neighbours to share the cost of protecting your common boundaries.

PIN THAT DOOR

A door opening to the outside can be removed simply by knocking the pins out of the hinges, but there is a solution to the problem:

1. Simply drill a hole into one flap of the hinge, and another in the corresponding position in the other flap. The hole in the flap on the doorjamb side should be a good depth, say 50 mm or so.
2. Insert a steel peg into that hole so that it protrudes about 10 mm when fully seated. Now, when the door is closed, the peg also sits snugly in the hole drilled in the hinge flap on the door side. Even if the hinge pins are removed, the door cannot be removed.

RODDY CLEVER

A similar idea is effective, but suitable only for those doors that you seldom, if ever, use:

1. Drill four holes in the door, and corresponding holes in the door-jamb. The depth of the holes in the door should be 80 mm, with a diameter of 12 mm. Those in the doorjamb, also 12 mm in diameter, should be 40 mm deep.
2. Cut four 85-mm lengths of 10-mm threaded rod and insert one each into the holes in the door – they should protrude about 5 mm or so, but still allow the door to open and shut properly.
3. Now use a knife blade to flick each rod in turn into the door-jamb. Each one, when fully home, should have about half its length in the door, and the other half in the jamb. A very positive lock – and difficult to spot.

KEEPING THE KEY IN THE SLOT

There might be occasions when you wish to leave a key in the lock. If so, you can still prevent anyone getting it from the other side. Use a short length of stiff wire to make up the gadget in the photograph. It hangs on the door handle, and the leg of the 'P' is long enough to pass through the hole in the key's grip. As it holds the key at an angle, it cannot be removed from the slot by manipulating it from the outside.

DON'T FORGET THE FLOOR AND ROOF

If your home has a suspended floor, have a movement sensor covering the underfloor space and, likewise, the roof space above the ceiling.

NOW I SEE YOU

If a door is in a recess, it might not be possible to see anyone lurking around the corner. Mount a car's rear-view mirror in a position that enables you to see around the corner.

BURGLAR BARS ARE GREAT, BUT . . .

Just as they can keep intruders out, so they can keep you in when you desperately need to get out, say in the event of a fire.

So, mount one set of burglar bars on hinges, with a couple of stout padlocks keeping it closed, and the key hanging nearby but out of sight and reach of someone trying to get in.

If you have a fire, you can unlock the bars and swing them aside.

STRUT YOUR STUFF

A cheap but very effective deterrent to intruders is a simple strut jammed under the door handle. It should stand at an angle of about 70 degrees to the vertical when in position. Make a little hollow at the top end so that it sits snugly against the bottom of the handle, and drill a hole through it for a piece of string to further reduce the possibility of its falling.

SECURE THE SLEEPING AREA

A security door installed in a passage leading to the sleeping area of the house is a useful addition to a home's security. A key should be close at hand, out of sight and reach of anyone approaching from the other side of the door. This measure, combined with the bars on hinges, could enable members of the family to escape in the event of a threatened attack.

A DOOR IS AS STRONG AS ITS WEAKEST PANEL

Some outside doors have relatively sturdy frames, but their panels might be somewhat flimsy. If this is the case, consider fixing a burglar bar to the inside of the door, to cover the panel.

Avoid leaving keys in locks, but when you do, this keeps them in.

A strut under the door handle enhances security.

THE DINING ROOM

In many homes nowadays the dining room is part and parcel of an open-plan kitchen/dining room/lounge area and modern homes tend to be smaller than those built some time ago. So space might be somewhat limited.

Having said that, the size and shape of your table – the dominant feature in the dining room – will be determined by the amount of entertaining you do, the shape of the room, and the space available.

Naturally, the more people you like to have around, the more guests you will need to seat. And since every person at the table will require about 650 mm of table side and about a metre between the side and the wall to enable the person to get into his seat easily, you will need a lot of space if you entertain a lot of people. So . . .

- If space is limited, consider a round dining-room table. In fact, consider one even if space is not that limited. Round tables allow every person at the table to get a clear view of everyone else, which is conducive to conversation. This shape of table also gives you a little more flexibility in how you arrange the other items of furniture, such as the sideboard. Since the round table has no 'side' as such, you have more choices. The limitation with this shape is that when you have extra guests and need to add another table, you can't! Well, not so easily, anyway.
- A square or rectangular table might be a better choice if your dining room is rectangular in shape and where the sideboard can comfortably occupy one of the shorter walls of the room.
- Chairs need to be comfortably padded, but need not necessarily be part of a set. If the latter is the case they should, however, comprise the same sort of materials and approximate the same sort of design characteristics; mixing wooden chairs with metal is not likely to create a harmonious impression.
- Lighting is important. Avoid having lights in positions where they will be in any-one's eyes. Subdued ceiling lighting will create an intimate effect, while a shielded light hung low over the centre of the table will help create the right atmosphere at the table. However, bear in mind that if you go this route, the centre light does tend to dictate where you position the table, though you can soften its influence with accent lighting directed at a picture on the wall, for instance.
- A plain white, cream or light pastel colour scheme is probably best.
- People spill! So carpeting is not an ideal choice of floor covering, except, perhaps, directly under the table. If so, and the carpet or rug is particularly striking, a glass table with place mats rather than a tablecloth will help provide another area of interest in the dining room. But back to people spilling . . . a tiled or wooden floor is easy to clean, and you should also select easy-to-clean materials for the surfaces of countertops and so on.
- If you have a serving hatch between the dining room and the kitchen, you might consider concertina or sliding doors to screen off the latter once the meal is served. After all, a scene comprising pots and pans needing a good clean tends to detract from the crystal glasses and heirloom dinner service – particularly when you're trying to impress the boss!

Opt for a round table if your space is limited – this shape also makes it much easier to position other pieces of furniture in a room.

Sliding doors are sometimes the weak link in home security, but bolting them down like this will make them far more secure.

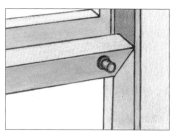

A sash window's security is enhanced very simply with just a nail.

PET'S DELIGHT

A pet flap mounted in a door allows your cats and dogs easy access to the home. But you might consider mounting burglar bars in this area too, positioned so that the flap can still swing freely but cannot be enlarged to allow entry by an outsider.

When it comes to a large dog, the opening it will require may be large enough to admit an intruder. That dog stays in or out! No flap!

MAKING SLIDING DOORS SAFER

Sliding doors can be made safer by ensuring that they cannot be lifted off their tracks. There are a couple of ways of preventing this:

- Drive a self-tapping screw into a sliding door just below the top frame, leaving enough of the screw protruding beyond the edge of the frame. Any attempt to lift the door will be foiled when the screw head makes contact with the frame.
- Drill an 8-mm hole through one surface of a short length of angle steel or aluminium and pop-rivet it to the bottom frame of the sliding door, as close to the floor as possible. Close the door, mark the drill point on the floor, and drill the hole for an 8-mm masonry anchor into the floor. Check for proper alignment and seat the masonry anchor shield firmly in position in the floor. Use a piece of scrap wood and the bolt to do this. Now, when you need to lock the door in position, close it, lock it, and turn the bolt home. It will hold the door very securely.

MAKING SASH WINDOWS SAFER

1. Drill a hole through both frames when the sash window is closed – the hole should be drilled at an angle of 20 degrees or so, so that the pin in it cannot be shaken out.
2. Now, when the window is shut, simply push a metal bar or nail of a suitable size into the hole. It will prevent the window being opened.

PEOPLE, PEOPLE WHO NEED PEEPHOLE

Most peepholes are fitted to a door at a convenient height for the adults and older children – but what about a younger child? He or she might not be able to see who's at the door, but if they can reach the handle, they can open it – even if you have stressed time and again that they should not. So, install a second peephole at eye-level height for them.

GET THE RIGHT MESSAGE ACROSS – 1

Don't have the message on your answering machine saying that you are out. The caller could be someone checking to see if the house is unoccupied.

Rather say, 'No one is available to answer the phone at the moment . . .'

Use a simple measure (see left) to lessen the security risk posed by sash windows.

Garage doors that open onto the street are vulnerable. Fit a pressure switch to the doors and connect it to a warning light in the home. If you forget to close your garage doors or someone opens them, the light will come on, warning you.

GET THE RIGHT MESSAGE ACROSS – 2

Most people who call and ask a series of questions are genuine and conducting a legitimate survey – or they're trying to get you to attend a time-share meeting.

Beware of a few things, however:

- Do not give details of credit card or bank account numbers. It sounds obvious, but some people have been enticed into giving these numbers and have lost money as a result.
- Do not give personal details regarding your day-to-day life – such as when you leave for work, who is present at home and when, and so on. You could be talking to someone who is planning to relieve you of your possessions.
- Do not give details of what you own – number of TVs, power tools, and so on – unless you are sure the caller is genuine.

BUSHWHACKED!

Keep areas near doors, windows, garages and main gates clear of bushes and tall plants – wrongdoers can use them for concealment.

SENSOR SENSE

There is a range of sensors available for just about every application. The key to enhanced security is providing a number of layers of protection – from a guard dog to different sensors in and around the home. It is best to have an expert come in and guide you, but here are some ideas that can help you decide:

- The cost of covering every area would be very high, so place sensors where they can do the most work. They should cover key areas, such as passages, doorways, stairways, windows and garage. One must cover the alarm control panel as well.
- One of the drawbacks of alarm systems is that they are switched off when we're at home, so consider buying a stand-alone battery-powered unit or two for the garage area, for example. These units are quite independent of the installed system and provide extra protection.
- Intruders hate light – so make it difficult for them. Install sensor-controlled lights in the carport and in selected spots so they cover areas of the home most likely to be targeted.
- Install panic buttons at strategic points in the home – in the kitchen and main bedroom, for instance. Those are areas in which one spends much of one's time.
- If you are going to have portable panic buttons as well, have a designated spot for each one when it is not being carried – there's nothing worse than having to search for one when you're in danger.

Take time to decide on where your sensors are positioned. This one covers the front door and lounge area.

- Arrange with the security company to check the system and each panic button, fixed or portable, once a month; if the battery in the latter is flat just when you need it, you have a problem.
- Outside remotes are fine, but you might not know if one on the other side of the house has been triggered, and once the intruder has seen that nothing happens when the lights go on, he'll figure it's safe to go ahead with his plans. Consider having an electrician connect a buzzer on an indicator board to each outside remote, or selected ones. Then you will have an audible alarm and be able to see at a glance which outside remote has been triggered.
- Keep each sensor's field clear of anything that can either trigger it or block its view.
- When out, don't leave notes on your door.
- When away, have your neighbours take a healthy interest in your home, and have them place a bag or two of rubbish outside your gate on collection day.
- Ask them to collect your post every day – a giveaway is a bulging postbox.
- Cancel newspaper and other deliveries such as bread and milk.
- Use timer switches to turn lights and the TV on and off during the first part of the evening – with a light going on much later for a little while just to show 'you're' awake!
- Take the 'multi' approach – a combination of sensors, from motion and heat sensors to pressure pads below windows, to magnetic sensors on doors and windows, and free-standing units as mentioned above . . . All of these combined with a sense of alertness (without becoming paranoid) can help keep you, your family and your home and possessions safe.
- Electric fencing around the perimeter of your property is a job for the experts. Nowadays, if an intruder is injured on your property or dies as a result of any action you take, **you** could end up in trouble. If you do have electric fencing installed, spend the money and have it around your entire property. Keep branches and foliage clear of it with regular pruning.

Don't put anything near a sensor that might block its field.

MOVING MADE EASY

A CHECK IN TIME

Before moving into a new home, just confirm that your present appliances fit where they are supposed to – dishwashers under counters, refrigerators behind doors, and so on. Sometimes the original owner has the kitchen remodelled around their existing appliances, such as the refrigerator, and your one might not fit.

There are some horrendous tales of mishaps at the hands of movers, but the fact of the matter is that in the vast majority of cases, moves are made with little trouble.

So here are some pointers:

- Timing – if you can move towards the middle of the month rather than at the end, you might be able to negotiate a better deal with the mover. You should also have a better chance of getting your mover of choice, because most people, when moving to a new job in another city or moving home, do so around the month end.
- Before selecting your mover, ask around. Chat to people who have recently moved into the area. Who moved them? What did it cost? Were they on time? Was there any damage to their goods? Did the movers have the damage repaired?
- Bear in mind that there's not much point asking a mover for names of clients – you're not likely to get the names of people who have been unhappy with their service.
- Major companies in the removals industry are jealous of their good name and can usually be relied upon to provide good service, but that should not preclude your considering the newer company that still has to make a name for itself and is consequently motivated to provide good service.
- The degree of professionalism on the part of the company is an indication of the sort of service you can expect. Clean transport, a professionally prepared quote on a purpose-made form, the amount of detail included in the quote; all these and more help to give you a good idea of the service you can expect.
- Insurance . . . It is a good idea to consider having your household items insured against loss or damage while in the care of the movers.

COLOURS AND NUMBERS FOR CLARITY

Save time by having cartons and furniture put in the right areas by the movers.

The easy way to do it is to colour-code each item with a sticker and put one of the same colour on the door of the relevant room. The movers just have to follow the colour trail and you're saved a lot of time carrying pieces to where you actually wanted them in the first place.

An alternative, using the same principle, is to give every item for a room the same main number. Everything marked with a large '1', for instance, is for the main bedroom, those marked '2' go to the bedroom next to the main one, those marked with a '4' go into the lounge, and so on.

HINT

A large box will be sufficient to contain a large variety of items, so make a list. Box 'A' contains crockery, ornaments and so forth, 'B' holds cups, saucers, and so on. Failing anything else, write the contents on the outside of the box, though this might not be a good idea from a security point of view.

MOVING HEAVY ITEMS

A platform of strong plywood, reinforced if necessary, mounted on casters, makes a very useful trolley on which to move heavy items of furniture and appliances. An alternative is to use an old carpet, pile side down. Place the appliance on that and drag it into position.

CUSHION THAT TV SCREEN

A cushion or pillow taped over your TV's screen will prevent its being damaged.

EASY-OPENING CARTONS

Save time and effort when unpacking – and prevent possible damage to a carton's contents from a knife blade. Lay a length of string along the middle of the tape when you're sealing cartons, and leave a little free at each end. Grip one end, pull up on the other, and you'll split the tape instantly.

A string down the middle ...

UNDOING KNOTS EASILY

Tie a short length of dowel into the middle of a knot when roping large items together. When you need to undo the knot, pull the dowel out and you will have a little more length to work with when loosening the knot.

Undo the knot easily – just use a dowel.

A SHATTERING SOLUTION

You hope that it won't happen, but it can – a mirror can be broken during transit. Reduce the risk of cuts from broken shards by applying a few strips of tape across a mirror before wrapping it in bubble wrap. If it should be broken, the tape will keep most of the pieces together.

A sheet of plywood, with a rope handle, make moving a heavy potplant easy.

garden

A beautiful garden need not be a big one, and there is no doubt that whatever its size, a beautiful garden will add to the enjoyment you derive from your home and enhance its aesthetic value – and even its real value should you wish to sell at some stage.

So, make the most of your garden – and we give you some tips on how to do that, from constructing simple retaining walls to paving with bricks and making water features.

You will also find some really crafty tips on making the most of your water and your swimming pool – including safety tips to ensure that your pool is a place for enjoyment, not tragedy.

We have also included information on plant varieties you may prefer not to have in your garden; in fact, in a couple of cases, it's best to avoid them like the plague!

Previous page: *As a quick and easy alternative to permanent paving (see p. 133), position loose concrete slabs or nonslip tiles at regular intervals on a layer of gravel, filling the spaces in between with gravel chips or pebbles.*
This page: *Absolute simplicity – a narrow water channel becomes a reflecting pool with soothing effect. For tips on creating your own water feature or pond, see pp. 147-150.*

CLEVER TRICKS

A SLIPPERY SOLUTION TO A RUSTY PROBLEM

Ever wondered what to do with that old engine oil? Here's the answer. Pour it into a container of sand; now derusting those garden tools and giving them a protective coat of oil every so often is easy. Simply push them into the container a few times.

YOUR GARDEN'S FOR THE BIRDS

Birds bring at least two benefits to a garden: many species make a meal of the insects that would otherwise make a meal of your plants, and birds are an attractive element in the garden.

So how do you attract them?

- A birdbath is a basic requirement. Birds love water.
- Water features are also attractive to them, but if you have young children, the birdbath route is the safer of the two.
- There is a wide variety of bird feeders available – usually plastic or wood.
- If you don't wish to go to the expense, even a 2-litre cool-drink bottle with a large hole cut in the side and filled with birdseed will do the trick.
- A dovecote will attract doves and pigeons and can also, like a birdbath or water feature, provide a focal point to the garden.
- Fruit trees that bear soft fruit – preferably varieties that you don't eat (you don't want to be in competition, do you?) – will attract birds.
- If you already have a tree that bears fruit you enjoy, and the birds enjoy the same variety, place peeled soft fruits such as oranges and apples on nails near a bird feeder to draw the birds away from your favourite.

Just a couple of points – put the birdbath well away from any cover the neighbourhood cat might use.

Also ensure that bird feeders and fruit you set out for the birds are well away from cover and at a height that makes it difficult for a cat to reach easily.

HERE COMES THE BRAAI . . .

It goes without saying that braaiing is a favourite pastime – but it can be quite expensive.

So, cut costs with these simple firelighters:
Fill a large coffee can with charcoal and pour in enough illuminating paraffin to cover the charcoal – though the pieces at the top will float.

Place the plastic lid on the can and leave it for a couple of days. The paraffin soaks into the charcoal, which then becomes a marvellous firelighter – at a fraction of the cost of the purchased variety. As you go through the charcoal, add more, and top up the paraffin from time to time.

Bottled birds.

Home-soaked firelighters, as cheap as you can get them.

CAUTION

Stick to illuminating paraffin as the flammable agent – don't use petrol or benzine.

If the coffee can, you can – make a perfect bed of coals, that is.

BECOME A GRIME FIGHTER

Yes, a braai is great – it's just a pity about the cleaning up afterwards.

Once the grill is cool, used a welder's steel brush to remove the worst of the deposit from the grill, then put it on a few newspapers and spray it liberally with oven cleaner. Leave it to soak in for a while, and then attack again with the steel brush. Most of the cooked-on deposits will be loosened and brush off easily.

Finish by cleaning the grill with kitchen detergent and rinsing off with clean water.

A PERFECT BED OF COALS? YOU CAN DO IT!

Purpose-made charcoal starter canisters are available, but you can achieve the same results with an ordinary coffee can.

1. Use a can opener to remove the base and cut about four V-shaped wedges in the sides – at about 90-degree intervals. Each wedge should be about 30 mm wide at the base, 10 mm wide at the top and about 40-50 mm high at the peak. Bend the wedges or flaps inwards to support the charcoal.
2. Place the can on a couple of crumpled pieces of newspaper. Fill the can to the brim with charcoal, and light the paper.
3. You should be able to remove the can with a pair of braai tongs after about 15 minutes. The coals will spread out into an even pile; spread it out a little more and add extra charcoal as required.

A series of rods incorporated in the wall give it a great deal of extra stability.

SOIL EROSION

MORTARLESS WALLS – DIRTY BUSINESS

Yes, it's a dirty business, but someone has to do it – stop slopes subsiding, that is.

HOW LOW CAN YOU GO?
■ Three or four courses of bricks, dry-packed and stepped back about 20 mm per course, are perfectly adequate to retain low slopes. The beauty of walls like these that do not use concrete in their construction, is flexibility.
■ If you decide at some stage that you'd like to change the course of the wall, it's easily done. However, to ensure a neat result, this type of wall's 'foundation' is important. Make sure it is level, and that the soil used to fill in any dips is well compacted.
■ Lay the entire first course as an initial step and cut and fill as required to get this course to lie as true as possible. Once that's done, you can lay the second and third courses.
■ A nice finishing touch, if you have used cored bricks (those with holes in the centre), is that you can fill the interior of the wall with potting soil and plant seeds along the top.
■ A similar result can be obtained with concrete blocks.

DON'T SPARE THE ROD
1. Reinforce a dry-packed block wall with steel rods for a stronger structure.
2. Step the blocks back as in the illustration and stagger them.
3. Then drive a series of rods down through the wall and the blocks' cells (the openings between the partitions in each block). Ensure the rods are driven well into the soil – at least half their length is ideal.
4. Finish the wall by pouring soil into its hollow core comprising the blocks' cells, and plant seeds or seedlings. After a while your wall should be a blaze of colour.

Again, the beauty is flexibility, but the drawback is the low height limitation. Purpose-made concrete retainers that interlock can be built to a substantial height. They are usually stepped back as well, but their special design makes for a strong wall. Their design also allows ample space for plants in the wall. But they are likely to be more expensive than either of the alternatives mentioned above.

CAUTION
Beware of building these walls too high. Generally limiting them to a maximum of four courses is best, and step each course back so that the wall leans into the slope.

Use plants to bind soil on slopes. Marigold seeds, for example, germinate quickly and their roots bind the top-soil area, while shrubs, with their deeper roots, bind the lower regions.

RETAINING WALLS

A retaining wall in which the bricks, blocks or stones are cemented into position is generally a project that needs careful consideration. For instance, local bylaws might limit the height of retaining walls, and other factors such as soil type, climate and proximity of a water source such as a stream or dam can affect the wall's design and construction.

Furthermore, unlike dry-packed walls, which allow the free passage of ground water, a wall incorporating concrete must have sufficient drainage – if it is inadequate, you could have a disaster.

The rule is: the higher the wall has to be, and the greater the slope behind, the stronger the wall and its foundation must be.

Generally, do not attempt a wall higher than a metre or so – and then get some expert advice first.

If you need a wall between 1,2 m and about 2 m, hire a qualified builder to do the job. For a wall over 2,4 m, bring in an engineer or architect.

SOIL EROSION – STOP IT!

Banked-up soil is particularly prone to erosion, especially if it is new and bare, and the prime object is to bind the soil as soon as possible.

■ Plant a number of shrubs that will, in time, become bushy. Their lower foliage traps some of the soil washed down the slope, and their deep roots will help to bind the soil.
■ In the meantime, however, the surface will be prone to erosion, so plant a liberal amount of seedlings and spread seeds, for example marigold seeds. They germinate within a couple of weeks and will help bind the soil near the surface. If necessary, back this measure up with 'sausages' of soil wrapped in shade cloth and pegged into position. Gum poles also work well, trapping the soil behind them.

You might still have some erosion, and the bank may subside a little, but these measures should keep most of the soil where you want it.

FENCES

PULLING THAT POST OUT

Repairing picket fences is quite straightforward, but it's getting old posts out that makes one sweat. So do it the easy way – well, the easier way . . .

1. Nail a block of wood securely to the base of the post and use a long beam – the longer the better – with a couple of bricks as a fulcrum, to lever the post out.
2. As it rises higher out of the ground, add another brick or two, to raise the pivot point.

Getting that post out is easier when you use a lever – the longer the better.

Shade-loving plants and a prominent water feature (see pp. 147-150) transform this small garden into a private sanctuary.

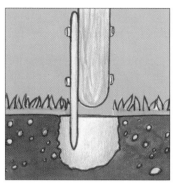

Bed a galvanised post in concrete and attach the wooden post to it – a good procedure in areas where the soil is usually wet.

HINT

Oil stains on paving look unsightly, but you can remove the worst by brushing dry cement over them or using your hand to roll cat litter over them and then brushing it off. Repeat as necessary. If you use cement, make sure that you remove all of it, if necessary with a vacuum – if it sets, it can become as big a problem as the original stains.

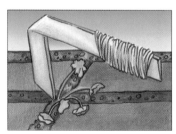

Weeds in paving are a headache, but this simple tool will help you get them out.

AND NOW TO ANCHOR A POST . . .

You don't need a huge amount of concrete to anchor a fence post or the pole for a washing line, for example.

1. Dig the hole and then drive three or four lengths of old pipe or steel bars into the surrounding soil. Each one need be only 600 mm or so, and driven in until only 100 mm projects into the hole.
2. Pack some loose stone chips into the bottom of the hole – but well below the projecting ends of the steel inserts – as this will improve drainage below the post. You have to be sure that the concrete will envelop the projecting ends.
3. Now fill the hole with the concrete and your post will stand firm.

A GATE WHERE YOU WANT IT

People often like to park their boat trailer or caravan in a part of the garden. So if you have a picket fence across the front of your property, make one section a 'drop-in' – it simply rests in joist hangers, available from building materials suppliers. When you need to get the trailer or caravan in or out, simply lift the fence section out of the way.

GET THOSE PICKETS LEVEL

Make identical picket fence sections the easy way, with a full sheet of plywood – which you will be able to reuse later for some other purpose.

1. Hot-glue a 44 mm × 44 mm length of SA pine along one edge of the sheet and a second one along one side – this forms a giant carpenter's square.
2. Then use hot glue to stick eight guides in position for the stringers – each one will rest between four guides, with their ends against the timber glued along the side of the sheet.
3. Now put the two stringers in position and start attaching your pickets to them, at the intervals you have decided upon.

PAVING

WEEDS IN PAVING, DIG THEM OUT

This simple tool is made from a piece of sheet steel about 25 mm wide – though the width is not crucial. Cut the end at an angle of 45 degrees or so, and bend the metal through 45 degrees as well, hammering it flat.

Wrap the handle end in a self-adhesive foam rubber strip, or cloth, to protect your hand, and start dragging those weeds.

The blade is thin enough to get between the bricks and will help you remove the roots as well – crucial if you are to remove the weeds permanently.

KILLING OFF THOSE WEEDS IN PAVING

The easy way is with boiling water. If possible, try to borrow a tea urn from your local school or the office so that you have a constant supply of boiling water. And start pouring.

The treatment is environmentally safe – except to the weeds – and is very economical.

A blowtorch is also effective, but it is more expensive as you will have to spend money on gas bottles.

PAVING WITH BRICKS

Paving with bricks is relatively straightforward. Begin with marking out the area to be paved – naturally it should be in proportion to the dimensions of the bricks you're using – and excavate the area to an even depth – the thickness of the brick, plus 50 mm or so for the sand bed below.

1. Peg two beams accurately in the excavation, ensuring they are at exactly the same level and parallel. Then make up a simple grader to level the sand bed.
2. This grader comprises two lengths of wood. The longer one rests on the two beams. The second, shorter one is short enough to fit between the two beams set to grade the sand to a depth that will put the top surfaces of the bricks about 5 mm above the level of the soil surrounding the area to be paved.
3. Spread sand in the excavation, grade it with the grader and use extra sand to fill in any low areas. Once you have finished grading the bed, compact it with a power vibrator. If you don't have one, then use a stamper to compact the bed. Wetting the bed with a light spray will assist the compaction. Pass the grader over the bed during the process so that you can spot and fill in low areas.
4. Once the bed is finished, lay the bricks (drop them into position from a height of about 20 mm; don't slide them over the surface, as you will displace the surface of the bed) course by course, and use a rubber mallet to tap them into place.
5. If you have a powered compactor, making a few passes over the bricks will seat them better. If you are concerned that the compactor might break any of the bricks, place a sheet of plywood between the compactor's base and the brick surface, to cushion the impact and spread the load.
6. Once the bricks have been laid and you are satisfied with the result, brush sand over them, spray lightly and allow to dry. Continue brushing sand over them and spraying until all the gaps between the bricks are filled.

Position the beams, ensuring that they are exactly level.

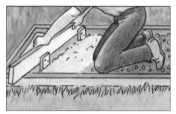

Excavate the area to be paved, add bedding sand, level it with the grader and compact it.

Drop each brick into position from a couple of centimetres – don't push it.

To finish, brush sand into the gaps between the bricks and spray lightly.

KEEPING MOLES OUT

The sight of a runner mole's tunnel snaking through a flowerbed is enough to get the average gardener excited. And the sight of a mound from a mole rat – which is vegetarian and will eat bulbs and roots – will encourage a similar emotion.

Don't despair.

Runner moles, also known as golden moles (apart from the rich terms gardeners might give them), eat insects and worms they find in the soil, so they do some good, but the trouble is they uproot small seedlings as they dig their tunnels.

To restrict them, line the edges of flowerbeds and your property too, if you can, with purpose-made solid edging buried in the soil to a depth of 300 mm or so. You might also try using fine chicken mesh, but this will rust in time and might also create problems when you're tending the bed. Another alternative is a length of black PVC damp-coursing.

Neither of these remedies is likely to work with mole rats, however, as their tunnels are deep underground and you will need to set traps, or use some of the more drastic methods that follow, in order to contain the threat.

DRIVING MOLES OUT AND GETTING RID OF THEM – PERMANENTLY!

You can buy mole traps which fit into their tunnels, or – because they are sensitive to smell – you can put your dog's garden contribution to good use by burying it in the tunnels here and there.

GIVE THEM THE WATERWORKS!

This is not exactly the best option in a country prone to droughts, but shoving a garden hose down the tunnel will get them moving.

EXHAUSTED ALL THE OPTIONS?

If you have tried everything, and before going to the expense of buying a repellent, try to get your car close to a tunnel or mound from a mole rat. Insert the end of the garden hose into the tunnel or mound, and jam the other end into the car's exhaust, using some cloth to seal it. Then let your car idle for a while.

With luck, you will achieve a more permanent solution to the problem – until the next mole arrives!

GETTING RID OF ANTS

There are various ant traps on the market, but you can also get rid of them by pouring boiling water into their nests. Talcum powder also deters them, as they dislike walking on powder. Powdered sulphur, borax and cream of tartar also repel them, and spreading any of these substances around entrance holes and among plants is an effective deterrent.

GIVE SNAILS A HAPPY EXIT . . .

Snails are attracted to beer (who isn't?), so if you don't wish to use snail bait and other products, place a shallow dish in the garden and fill it with beer – the snails climb up, fall in and drown.

. . . OR A QUICKER ONE

Ducks love snails and will make short work of them. If you can keep a couple of ducks, subject to your existing pets, do so. They will keep snails and some other pests under control and all they need in return is normal feeding and care, and a smallish plastic paddling pool for them to swim in.

PLANTS THAT REPEL PESTS

Save yourself time and money – use plants to repel some of the pests that plague your garden:

- Garlic – no joy when on someone's breath – is just as repellent to greenfly. Plant it between your roses to discourage this pest.
- Marigolds – deter whiteflies.
- Nasturtiums – also deter whiteflies.

And some other methods:

- Kill mites with a mist spray of buttermilk.
- Wood ash sprinkled around the plants will help control onion maggots and bean beetles.
- Fennel, sage, buckwheat and Queen Anne's lace attract hover flies, ladybirds, lace wings and parasitic wasps and flies – all of which are beneficial in the garden. Ladybirds, for instance, feed on aphids.

Using plants to repel pests makes sense.

POISONOUS PLANTS, DANGEROUS PLANTS

Some of the most deadly hazards in nature are also some of the most attractive, and this is true of a wide variety of garden plants as well. All of some plants, and parts of others – the fruit, for instance – are poisonous.

Naturally, we don't go around putting bits of plants into our mouths, but sap can get into our eyes, we prick ourselves on thorns, and children are attracted to berries and fruits – and you could have an emergency on your hands.

There are other plants that, though not poisonous, can be dangerous – such as sisal planted at the bottom of a grassy bank.

Here are just some of the plants you need to watch out for. In each case, part of the plant may be poisonous, or all of it. For safety's sake, assume the whole plant is dangerous and get rid of it.

House and garden plants that are poisonous and pose a danger to children and pets are:

- Amaryllis
- Birds of paradise
- Bushman's poison
- Castor oil plant
- Dieffenbachia
- English ivy
- Tobacco
- Iris
- Lantana
- Moonflower
- Narcissus
- Succulent euphorbia
- Jerusalem cherry
- Syringa
- Angel's trumpet
- Black nightshade
- Caladium
- Daffodil
- Elephant's ear
- Foxglove
- Hyacinth
- March lily
- Monstera
- Oleander
- Philodendron
- Thorn apple
- Fly agaric mushroom

Delightful to look at, but dangerous.

HINT
Poisons are available to kill off tree stumps and root systems, but diesel also works well. Drill a number of large holes into the stump and fill them with diesel. Top up as necessary.

THERE'S AN ALIEN IN YOUR GARDEN...

Legislation aimed at ridding the country of alien plants covers a wide variety commonly found in suburban gardens. Trying to sell your home with aliens in the garden could also be a problem.

So why not get rid of them while you have the chance to do it in your own time and re-establish your garden.

Here are just some of them you need to be aware of, but for a complete list and expert advice, consult a reputable nursery.

The following plants are deemed Category 1 and must be removed and destroyed. No trade in these plants is permitted:

- Silver wattle
- Lebbeck tree
- Indian shot
- Red cestrum
- Hakea
- Red ginger lily
- Kahli ginger lily
- Seed-producing lantana – all species
- Banana poka, bananadilla
- Wax tree
- Spanish broom
- Yellow bell
- Mexican ageratum
- Giant/Spanish reed
- Yellow/orange cestrum
- Pampas grass
- White ginger lily
- Yellow ginger lily
- Cat's claw creeper
- New Zealand Christmas tree
- Oleander
- Fountain grass
- Bugweed
- Chinese and pink tamarisk
- Yellow oleander

These Category 2 plants can only be grown under controlled conditions – such as for agricultural or forestry purposes:

- Silver wattle
- Port Jackson willow
- Beefwood
- Guava
- Weeping willow
- Australian blackwood
- Sisal hemp
- Horsetail tree
- Castor oil plant

Category 3 plants, of which the following are some examples, are permitted to grow where they already exist, but no propagation, new planting or trade is allowed. This is a partial list:

- Bailey's wattle
- Pearl acacia
- Orchid tree
- Loquat
- Jacaranda
- Mulberry
- Yellow firethorn
- Rose apple
- Toon tree
- Pepper wattle
- Butterfly orchid tree
- Cotoneaster
- Morning glory
- Syringa
- Chinese guava
- Brazilian pepper tree
- Tipu tree
- Sword fern

An alien in your garden could present a problem in the future. This is just a small sampling of listed aliens. Chat to your local nursery for further information.

Try the pipe trick to get water to the roots with no wastage.

Trouble-free watering starts with a bottle.

Drill a few holes first, check the spread, and then drill more if necessary.

Let us spray – with a bottle.

SAVE WATER – GROUP THEM

Grouping plants with similar water needs makes sense. After all, when one that requires only a little is next to one that needs a lot, one or the other – or both – will get an amount that is not the ideal. Chat to your local nurseryman and devise a few lists of plants that will provide contrasting colours, shapes and textures, and require the same level of watering.

SAVE WATER – USE THE POT PLANT PIPE TRICK

Sink a length of pipe into the soil next to a plant and top it up when you are watering the garden – you'll get the water straight to where it's needed, the roots, with minimal evaporation.

KEEP IT MOIST – GIVE THAT SEEDLING OR SLIP SOME BOTTLED WATER

Need to keep soil around a slip or seedling moist? Fill a 2-litre cool-drink bottle and up-end it in the soil next to the plant. As the soil dries, a gap will form at the bottleneck, air will enter, and a little water will be released. This will seal the gap until the soil dries again. Virtually no wastage, and trouble-free watering for a few days.

WHAT A COOL IDEA

A plastic cool-drink bottle makes a quick and easy substitute when you can't find your sprinkler attachment. Make a 12-mm hole in the top of the cap of a 2-litre cool-drink bottle and push the insert from a hose connector into it, and connect the hose to it. Use a drill or heated nail to make a few holes in one side of the bottle (not around the whole circumference), connect it to the hose and lie it on its side in the garden. Check if the spray covers the area you want it to, and make more holes if necessary.

USE PLANTS TO HIDE UNSIGHTLY FEATURES

There's more to simply planting something, anything, in front of a feature you'd like to obscure. Part of the challenge is to break up the shape of the feature – this is one of the keys to camouflage.

So, don't necessarily plant a creeper to grow up the wall, and nothing else; all you will end up with is a very regular expanse of creeper – and a good idea of what's behind.

Try for a natural result that will combine the creeper, if that is your choice, with a couple of taller plants – placed off-centre – and a shrub or bush off to one side. All of these, when mature, will break up the shape of the feature.

PLANTING FOR PERSPECTIVE

Use plants to create an impression of length, or the opposite.

■ If you wish to create depth in a short garden, position larger plants in the foreground and progressively shorter plants towards the boundary at the end of the garden. You can enhance the illusion by narrowing flowerbeds down the sides of the garden. They need not follow a straight line, but if the overall result is to make them progressively narrower, they will seem longer and make the garden boundary at the far end seem further away.

■ The opposite result will be obtained with a longer, narrower garden that you wish to 'shorten'. If you have shorter plants closer to the house and taller ones further away, with flowerbeds becoming progressively wider the further they are from the home, you will tend to bring the end of the garden closer.

Remember that perception is reality!

PAINTING BEHIND TRELLISES – ALL FALL OUT

Take the hassle out of painting the wall behind a trellis – attach it to the wall with eyebolts. The bottom of the trellis is attached to the wall with two cup hooks that sit in eyebolts in the wall. The top is also hooked onto eyebolts and secured with a single shield bolt and butterfly nut.

When you need to paint behind it, use a couple of lengths of cord to allow the trellis to hang away from the wall. Paint behind it as planned, and once the paint is dry, reattach it firmly in position.

No more hassles with painting behind a trellis.

SWIMMING POOLS

FIND THAT LEAK!

This method works for any pool, whatever the material used in its construction – and you won't even have to get into the water.

1. Tie a length of aquarium pipe to a dowel.
2. Put a couple of fragments of potassium permanganate into a syringe, fill it with water and dissolve the grains.
3. Connect the syringe to the tube and depress the plunger, filling the tube with the stained water from the syringe.
4. Now place the end of the tube near the suspected leak, and depress the syringe plunger a little. The stained water is clearly visible and you will be able to see it being drawn towards the leak.

Just ensure that the potassium permanganate crystals have all dissolved completely, as any that land on the bottom of the pool will leave a brown stain. It should disappear eventually, but why run the risk?

Fill the tube with the potassium permanganate mix and move the tube to where you think the leak may be.

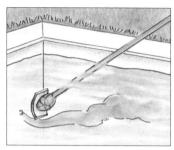

When the stained water streams away, there's the leak.

So, is it leaking? Ensure that the water level in the drum matches the pool level precisely when you start the test.

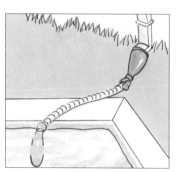

It won't win any prizes for beauty, but in a drought-prone land like this, water is water – and it's better in your pool than down the drain.

FIX THAT LEAK!

There is a range of products on the market to repair pools and it is simply a matter of following the instructions. The following method works on leaks in vinyl pools – and is a useful trick to know if a leak develops in winter when the water is too cold for a dip.

1. A leak in a vinyl pool is sealed with a patch. Wrap a large amount of cloth around the end of a dowel until it looks like a giant ear bud. To the end of the pad attach a short length of masking tape that has been looped, adhesive side outwards.
2. Prepare the patch and place it on the end of the pad, where the masking tape will hold it in position.
3. Now, standing as close as you can to directly above the leak – to reduce the problems caused by refraction – lower the patch towards the leak and once directly above it, place it in position.

The masking tape will probably remain on the patch when you pull the pad away, but don't worry, it will soon come loose and will be picked up by your pool cleaner.

SO, IS IT LEAKING?

What seems like a leak in a pool might not always be, but to be more certain, you can use a 200-litre drum to check.

1. Place a drum in the pool (put it on a sheet of plastic to prevent any rust on the rim discolouring the bottom of the pool) and top it up to match the water level in the pool exactly.
2. Leave it there for a few days, and avoid using the pool at all as splashing will, naturally, affect the final result. If, after a few days, the pool water is significantly below that in the drum, you probably have a leak.

KEEP THAT POOL TOPPED UP

Keeping a pool topped up in a country like this that is prone to droughts can present a problem, so make the most of any rain.

1. Slip a short length of motorcar inner tube over the end of the gutter downpipe (your local retread outlet should have some spare tubes) and secure it in position.
2. Slip the end of a continuous length of pool cleaner pipe into the other end of the inner tube and secure it firmly in position. You can get a tight seal if you glue a length of PVC pipe into the end of the pool cleaner pipe and use a Jubilee clip to ensure a tight seal between the tyre tube and the PVC insert.
3. Tie a pantihose leg over the other end of the cleaner pipe and put it into the pool. Now, when it rains, your pool will get a welcome fill-up and the pantihose leg will trap the debris.

NOTE: It's a good idea to keep your gutters clean to reduce the amount of debris.

A swimming pool requires careful and constant maintenance to keep it crystal clear. See pp. 141-144 for numerous hints that will help you save both money and water.

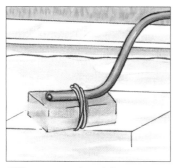

Why waste electricity to drain excess water from your pool when some pipe and a brick will do the same?

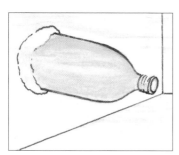

Getting that concentrated algaecide right where you want it.

DRAINING OFF THE EXCESS THE EASY WAY

When the pool is overfull and the weir is covered, you may wish to drain off the excess. If your property is on even a slight slope, you can do it easily without pumping it out and having to wait until the water reaches the right level.

1. Tie the end of a continuous length of pool cleaner pipe to a brick and place it on the top step. Use a second brick or other item to set the **top** of the end of the pipe to the depth to which you want the pool drained.
2. Have a second pair of hands hold the brick and pipe in place, and push the entire pipe below the surface to fill it completely with water.
3. With both ends of the pipe blocked with the palm of a hand, drag the free end away from the pool and down the slope. Lay it on the ground and remove the hand. At the same time, your helper takes his hand off the end in the pool. The water will now siphon out of the pool until the desired level is reached; the moment the top of the pipe is able to draw in air, the siphon action stops, and the pool stops draining.

GET RID OF ALGAE

There is a range of excellent products to rid a pool of every type of algae, but occasionally you come across a particularly resistant patch. Try rubbing it with a solid pool pill, but if that doesn't work, a more drastic solution might work.

1. Cut the base off a 2-litre plastic cool-drink bottle and shape the cut end to match the pool contour. Line the rim with Prestik and place the bottle firmly over the patch, ensuring the Prestik seals the edge properly.
2. Fill a large syringe with a pure algaecide and slip a short length of aquarium tube over the nozzle. The tube should be long enough to reach the surface to be treated, when the syringe is at the top of the bottle, so that the algaecide is deposited as close to the infestation as possible.
3. Now, slowly depress the plunger to expel the algaecide, withdraw the tube and put the cap on the bottle.

The strong solution is now confined in the sealed bottle and will give the algae a far heftier kick.

POOL SAFETY

There is no surer way of having a pool turned into a rose garden than having a tragedy. And there are few things that can occur more quickly than a tragedy.

Two precautions too many are better than one too few, and you should bear in mind that owning a pool is a responsibility. Even if you don't have children, or they are grown up, you still owe it to your community to ensure adequate safety precautions are in place. So:

■ Ensure that the pool area is fully fenced with an approved design of fencing which a child cannot climb over, under or through, and which is at least 1,2 m high.
■ The gate should be self-closing and self-locking.
■ Do not leave anything near the fence that a child can use to scale it.
■ Consider a pool net in addition to the fencing.
■ If you feel the fencing most commonly used doesn't suit your pool and decide on wooden picket fencing instead, the stringers should be on the inside so that they do not give a child a foothold.
■ If going for an alternative type of fencing, check with your local authority first – they might specify what can be used.
■ Ensure the base of the fence is close enough to the ground along its whole length to prevent children getting under it, and top up areas where soil has been eroded. You might consider laying a line of rocks along the base and cementing them into place. Or use hollow-core concrete blocks on the inside of the fence to block any possible entrances; filling the blocks with soil and planting flowers in them will create a splash of colour along the fence.
■ Consider a floating splash detector as well.
■ Keep the gate to the pool locked and ensure that the key is always kept in one place, and as close as possible to the pool gate – you don't want to be searching for the key. A good alternative is a securely tightened quick link, which can be unscrewed in a couple of seconds.
■ Never allow anyone – including yourself – to swim alone; accidents do happen.
■ Ensure that the pool surrounds and steps are nonslip.
■ Even if you enjoy swimming in the nude and have high barriers around the pool, keep some fields of view open, for example from the lounge or kitchen – you never know when an accident might occur.
■ Practise the procedures you might have to adopt in the event of an accident so that you know immediately what to do.
■ Whatever you do, don't panic.

HINT

Pool nets are available in a variety of mesh sizes, right down to relatively closely woven leaf nets. The latter are not safety nets, per se, but they will prevent small pets and wildlife such as skinks from falling into the pool. As an additional safety measure, you can also leave a body board or plank of wood floating in the pool – either may provide a refuge for anything that has fallen in.

A quick link, tightened sufficiently, will be a barrier to small children, but adults will be able to get into the pool area quickly, without having to look for the key.

Different shapes, levels and textures have been used to create this striking water feature in a private courtyard.

WATER FEATURES

ABOUT WATER FEATURES . . .

Before taking a look at water features, bear in mind that a fishpond in the garden is as big a hazard for small children as a swimming pool, so think twice about having a water feature in the garden if you have a small child.

After all, one of the aims of having a feature is to bring beauty to the garden – and whereas a fence around a swimming pool looks fine, one around a fishpond does not, which means you probably won't put one around it.

Some points to bear in mind when considering a pond or water feature:

- Rocks of the same colour should be used around ponds, and they should match those in the rest of the garden – they will jar if they have a very different colour or texture.
- Having to remove leaves from the water will be less of a chore if you choose your plants carefully or position the pond well away from plants that shed their leaves.
- A pond should be about twice as wide as its fountain to reduce water loss, but bear in mind that a fountain will increase the loss. Generally, the larger the pond, the better the fountain will look.
- Positioning overhanging plants at some places around a smaller pond will make it seem bigger, as the water will 'disappear' under the plants and create an impression of greater size.
- If you are fortunate enough to have a stream running through your property, you will probably be able to create an informal pond that will not require sealing. Plants that like the soggy conditions around such ponds include arum lilies, peacock flowers, broom reeds, dwarf glory bushes, river lilies, elephant's ear, umbrella grass and papyrus. Planting these around a pond will give you a rich mix of textures and foliage.
- Fish will need shade, and water lilies are a good choice – they love still water and sun.
- If you intend keeping fish that can grow to a substantial size, such as koi, you should allow for a filtration system near the pond.
- Also bear in mind that a pump and fountain will require electricity. Before committing yourself to this, check with a qualified electrician and have it installed professionally. If you get it wrong, you could put lives in danger, and if you decide to sell your home and you haven't used the correct materials or methods, you will have to have your work corrected before you can sell your house.
- By far the safest route to take is to use a pump that works via a transformer, which reduces the mains power to 12 volts. This won't put anyone's life in danger.
- Design the pond to suit your house and garden. A round or square shape looks best in a formal or semiformal garden, while the natural look with a rock and waterfall suits an informal garden.

Fish will need a mix of sun and shade.

- Ever tried getting a pot plant out of a pot without losing half the soil? Try this: when potting a seedling or slip, line the pot with some plastic sheeting, not forgetting to make a few drainage holes in the base. When you need to repot the seedling, just lift it out and peel off the sheet. Nothing could be simpler.
- Keep stress to a minimum when repotting plants. Place the existing pot in the new one and pack the potting mixture around it. Now carefully withdraw the pot, tap it loose and place the plant and its root system in the depression you created. Apart from the thickness of the pot walls, you will have a perfect fit, and the plant's root system will be able to develop without a hitch.
- If you don't use gardening gloves, use soap to keep those nails clean: scrape your nails along a bar of cheap soap before you begin gardening. You won't get any dirt trapped under them, and a simple scrub gets rid of the soap in a moment.

CLEVER USES FOR PLASTIC SHEETS

You can use plastic sheets in a number of applications in and around the home:

- The 250-micron black plastic available from hardware stores makes a very good lining for a fishpond or water feature in the garden.
- If a roof tile cracks, remove the pieces and wrap the tile in a sheet of plastic large enough to wrap around it completely, with the ends meeting on the tile's underside. Now put the tile back in position; its weight will keep the plastic from coming loose and you'll have a leak-proof solution until you can replace the tile with a new one.
- In sandy soils, watering your garden can take more water than you'd like because it simply soaks away. But you can use a plastic sheet to make a garden bed that will retain water a lot longer so that the plants can absorb more of it. Dig out the bed and line it with a single sheet of plastic. Now fill it with the soil mixture you have made up. Trim off the excess plastic so that when the bed is complete, none shows. Now simply use a garden fork to make a number of drainage holes, well spaced across the area of the bed. Rather make too few holes at first, and then check how long the bed retains moisture. If you find it stays wet too long, make a few more holes, but be circumspect – too many holes and you've probably wasted your time as the bed will dry out too quickly.
- Leaking bucket? As a temporary measure, line it with a plastic sheet large enough to overhang the rim completely. It might not look pretty, but it will give you a waterproof container until you can buy a new bucket.

- Position the pond where you can see and enjoy it.
- There is a wide range of pumps available and you need to select the one that will suit the size of the pond. Too powerful a pump in a small pond will disturb the water and the fish, while too weak a pump will not circulate the water sufficiently.
- If you construct a pond and line it with concrete, you will be able to include a tint in the mix to colour the concrete. However, allow the completed pond mix to cure properly after construction – if you move your fish in too soon they are very likely to die. Preparing the pond will mean filling and draining it to get rid of any contaminants that could harm the fish – consult the experts before starting on a project like this.
- Use a pond or water feature to fill a corner of the garden that you might not otherwise make use of.
- A bridge made of two railway sleepers is a very effective and durable addition to a pond, and allows you a level platform from which to feed or view the fish.
- Beware of herons and cats: both might be attracted, and if so, you may have to string a net across the pond to prevent fish being lost.

- Sorry to put you off, but snakes, too, are attracted to water, particularly when the weather is hot and dry, so bear this in mind when considering a pond or water feature.
- Incorporating a fountain or waterfall in a pond or feature in which you will keep fish is a good idea. Not only will either one of these greatly enhance the feature's appearance, but they will also aerate the water.

BUILDING A SIMPLE POND

Building a simple pond is not a difficult task and a good place to start, since this version will give some experience and be impermanent enough that you can disassemble it and try again.

Hence, the materials are cheap, the shape is up to you and the effect can be rather good, despite the low cost. You'll be using 250-micron black plastic sheeting (it comes in 4-m wide sheets) from your local building merchant, and bricks for the edging.

The pond is also semirecessed, which saves you a lot of digging.

Here's how you do it:

1. Select a position for the pond.
2. Trace out the shape with string and dig a shallow hole, about 300 mm deep, piling the excavated soil evenly around the perimeter of the pond. Bear in mind that as the plastic is available in a maximum of 4 m wide, the maximum width of your pond, plus the sides, must take account of this. As regards length, you have a free hand.
3. Clear the hole of any sharp rocks or roots.
4. Even out the ridge of soil around the perimeter to form a raised, level foundation for the blocks or bricks. To confirm it is level, place a spirit level on a straight piece of wood and check the ridge at various points.
5. Lay the brick courses, but no more than two or three deep, as the weight of water could be too great for anything higher.
6. Smooth the inner surface as much as possible and lay a doubled sheet of the plastic over the construction. There must be an equal overlap on both sides, and you should do a quick check to ensure that when it is flat against the base across its whole width, the edges still reach the top of the brick courses.
7. Start filling the pond, smoothly folding the plastic where necessary for a neat result. Be careful, though – the easiest place to work at this stage is standing in the pond, but watch out, the plastic will be slippery.

Take care to keep the width of the pond within limits.

Do not use more than two or three layers of bricks for the edge.

8. Fill the pond to a few centimetres short of the top, fold the excess plastic over the top course of bricks and trim off the excess. Now add your last brick course, which will hold the plastic in place and hide it with an attractive finish. Continually check the bricks for any shifting. If any do, drive steel rods straight down into the soil below and the original ground to help hold them in position.

9. The capacity of the pond will largely determine the size of the pump, and to know the capacity, you will need to measure the flow: note the time it takes the hose to fill a 20-litre container, and then note the time it takes to fill the pond. From there it is a simple calculation to find its capacity.

10. Let your local pet shop guide you in the type and size of pump that will best suit your pond.

11. Whether you're setting up a fountain or waterfall, put the pump as close as you can to it, with a large-diameter hose from the far end of the pond to the pump inlet. This will ensure that the pump will circulate the water, rather than simply rotating a small area of it.

12. Set up your power supply to the pump or, as suggested earlier, have an electrician do it for you. In any event, ensure that the power cord is well protected in a PVC conduit and buried deep enough for safety – and make a point of noting exactly where it runs.

13. Carefully add the water plants of your choice to the pond, and plants to the surround, ensuring when doing the latter that you do not disturb your pond's foundation bank.

14. Once satisfied, add fish. Sit back and enjoy.

The completed pond: an attractive addition to your garden.

index

useful addresses

NOTE: Bear in mind that contact details can change.

MANUFACTURERS/ SUPPLIERS

PAINTS

DULUX
Website: http://www.dulux.co.za/
GAUTENG
8 Juyn Street, Alrode, Alberton 1449
Tel: (011) 817 3302
Toll free (in SA): 0800 111 017
Fax: (011) 861 1422
E-mail: info@dulux.co.za
For Dulux stockists in your area:
http://www.dulux.co.za/decorate/
stockframe.htm

PLASCON
Website: http://www.plascon.co.za/
EASTERN CAPE
4 Bedford Street, Neave Township,
Port Elizabeth 6020
Tel: (041) 43 4100
Fax: (041) 43 4596
GAUTENG
Barlow Park, Katherine Avenue, Sandton
2148
Tel: (011) 301 4600
Fax: (011) 448 1011
KWAZULU-NATAL
1236 South Coast Road, Mobeni Durban
4052
Tel: (031) 451 3200
Fax: (031) 451 3408
WESTERN CAPE
12 Packer Avenue, Epping 2, Cape Town
7460
Tel: (021) 534 6151
Fax: (021) 534 3791
E-mail: advice@plascon.co.za
Retailers in your area: http://www.plascon.
co.za/frames_paint_partners.html

WONDERCOAT
Website: http://www.wondercoat.co.za/
Contact: http://www.wondercoat.
co.za/contactus/contactus.html
Stockists: http://www.wondercoat.co.za/
stockists/stockists.html

VADEK
Website: http://www.cia.co.za/advert/
househld/vadek.htm
BLOEMFONTEIN
Tel: (051) 435 5621
Fax: (051) 307 144

CAPE TOWN
Tel: (021) 511 9330
Fax: (021) 511 6667
DURBAN
Tel: (031) 206 1007
Fax: (031) 705 2726
EAST LONDON
Tel: (043) 435 218
Fax: (043) 438 555
JOHANNESBURG
Tel: (011) 392 7850
Fax: (011) 392 7900
PORT ELIZABETH
Tel: (041) 547 603
Fax: (041) 571 563
PRETORIA
Tel: (012) 379 4319
Fax: (012) 804 1123

TOOLS

ATLAS COPCO/ALLIANCE TOOLS
CAPE TOWN
Tel: (021) 552 2073/76/81
Fax: (021) 551 2947
DURBAN
Tel: (031) 700 4575
Fax: (031) 700 5705
EAST LONDON
Tel: (043) 743 0260
Fax: (043) 743 0235
JOHANNESBURG
Tel: (011) 821 9000
Fax: (011) 821 9106/7
PORT ELIZABETH
Tel: (041) 451 2023/2718
Fax: (041) 451 4703

BLACK & DECKER
Website: http://www.blackanddecker.com/
CAPE TOWN
Tel: (021) 511 0680
DURBAN
Tel: (031) 305 3222
JOHANNESBURG
Tel: (011) 448 2300

BOSCH/SKIL
CAPE TOWN
Tel: (021) 511 8816
DURBAN
Tel: (031) 328 535
Fax: (031) 328 535
JOHANNESBURG
Tel: (011) 651 9600
Fax: (011) 651 9825

LASHER
CAPE TOWN
Tel: (021) 511 9964
Fax: (021) 511 5596
JOHANNESBURG
Tel: (011) 825 1100
Fax: (011) 825 6822

MAKITA
Website: http://www.makitatools.com/
CAPE TOWN
Tel: (021) 932 0568
Fax: (021) 932 3006
DURBAN
Tel: (031) 252 346
Fax: (031) 252 013
JOHANNESBURG
Tel: (011) 873 1260
Fax: (011) 873 1689

METABO
(industrial tools only)
CAPE TOWN
Tel: (021) 593 0950
Fax: (021) 593 0952
DURBAN
Tel: (031) 312 0242
Fax: (031) 312 0271
JOHANNESBURG
Tel: (011) 372 9600
Retail sales to public stockists:
Makro
Website: http://www.makro.co.za/

RECORD TOOLS
JOHANNESBURG
Tel: (011) 422 2340
Fax: (011) 422 4151
E-mail: sales@recordtools.co.za

RYOBI
JOHANNESBURG
Tel: (011) 444 3320
Fax: (011) 444 3565

ORGANISATIONS AND ADVISORY BODIES

AUTOMOBILE ASSOCIATION OF SOUTH AFRICA
Website: http://www.aasa.co.za/
Head Office, Dennis Paxton House,
Kyalami Grand Prix Circuit, Allandale
Road, Kyalami Midrand 1685

Postal address: PO Box 596,
　Johannesburg 2000
Tel: (011) 799 1000
Fax: (011) 799 1960

AA QUICK GUIDE TELEPHONE NUMBERS
**The nation-wide AA Emergency Rescue
Service Number**
Toll-free: 0800 01 01 01 (24 hours a day,
　seven days a week)
AA Mayday Medical Emergency Rescue
Toll-free: 0800 033 007 (24 hours a day,
　seven days a week)
AA Plus Extended Membership Service
Toll-free: 0800 111 997 (24 hours a day,
　seven days a week)
AA Membership Enquiries
(011) 799 1001 (08:00-16:30, Mon-Fri)
AA Travel Services
(011) 799 1400 (08:00-17:00, Mon-Fri)
AA Road Report
(011) 799 1400 (08:00-16:30, Mon-Fri)
AA Legal Services
(011) 799 1300 (08:00-17:00, Mon-Fri)
Technical Advice
(011) 799 1963 (08:00-16:30, Mon-Fri)
Vehicle Running Costs
(011) 799 1964 (08:00-16:30, Mon-Fri)
AA Insurance Services
0861 01 02 03 (08:00-20:00, Mon-Fri)
New AA Member Enrolments
0861 111 994 (08:00-16:30, Mon-Fri)
AA Auto Finance
Toll-free: 0800 200 100 (08:00-20:00,
　Mon-Fri; 08:00-12:00, Sat)
AA Impact Accident Management
　(Enquiries)
(011) 799 1616 (08:30-16:30, Mon-Fri)
AA Car Care Warranty (Enquiries)
(011) 799 1608 (08:30-16:30, Mon-Fri)

THE AA AUTOSHOP
http://www.aasa.co.za/contact/
　contactframe.html

THE AA TECHNICAL AND ROADWORTHY CENTRES
http://www.aasa.co.za/contact/
　contactframe.html

BUILDING INDUSTRIES FEDERATION OF SA
Website: http://buildnet.csir.co.za/bifsa/
　Members.htm

CORPORATE MEMBERS

MASTER BUILDERS ASSOCIATION BOLAND
PO Box 488, Paarl 7620
Tel: (021) 863 3330
Fax: (021) 863 3331

CAPE PENINSULA MASTER BUILDERS & ALLIED TRADE ASSOCIATION
PO Box 382, Rondebosch 7700

Tel: (021) 685 2625
Fax: (021) 685 2622

EAST CAPE MASTER BUILDERS ASSOCIATION
PO Box 7086, Newton Park 6055
Tel: (041) 365 1835
Fax: (041) 364 1676

CONSTRUCTION INDUSTRIES ASSOCIATION FREE STATE
PO Box 542, Welkom 9460
Tel: (057) 352 6269
Fax: (057) 353 2402

GAUTENG MASTER BUILDERS ASSOCIATION
PO Box 4841, Halfway House 1685
Tel: (011) 805 6688
Fax: (011) 805 6718

KWAZULU-NATAL MASTER BUILDERS & ALLIED INDUSTRIES ASSOCIATION
PO Box 582, Westville 3630
Tel: (031) 266 7070
Fax: (031) 266 6348

NORTH BOLAND MASTER BUILDERS ASSOCIATION
PO Box 13, Worcester 6849
Tel: (023) 342 6964
Fax: (023) 347 1907

NORTHERN CAPE MASTER BUILDERS AND ALLIED TRADES ASSOCIATION
PO Box 819, Kimberley 8300
Tel: (053) 831 1845
Fax: (053) 832 1368

AFFILIATED & ALLIED MEMBERS

ASSOCIATION OF ARCHITECTURAL ALUMINIUM MANUFACTURERS OF SOUTH AFRICA (AAAMSA)
PO Box 15852, Lyttelton 0140
Tel: (012) 664 5570
Fax: (012) 664 5659

THE ELECTRICAL CONTRACTORS ASSOCIATION (SOUTH AFRICA) (ECA)
PO Box 9683, Edenglen 1613
Tel: (011) 392 0000
Fax: (011) 974 9402

INDUSTRIALISED BUILDING ASSOCIATION (SA) (IBASA)
PO Box 1619, Halfway House 1685
Tel: (011) 805 1985
Fax: (011) 315 1644

MASTER MASONS & QUARRY OWNERS ASSOCIATION (SOUTHERN AFRICA)
PO Box 488, Paarl 7620
Tel: (021) 863 3330
Fax: (021) 863 3331

CONSTRUCTION INDUSTRIES FEDERATION OF NAMIBIA
PO Box 1479, Windhoek 9000
Tel: 09264 61 230 028
Fax: 09264 61 224 534

SOUTH AFRICAN REFRIGERATION & AIR CONDITIONING ASSOCIATION (SARACCA)
PO Box 75912, Gardenview 2047
Tel: (011) 622 3890
Fax: (011) 622 2534

REFRACTORIES CONTRACTORS ASSOCIATION (REFCA)
PO Box 3114, Vanderbijlpark 1900
Tel: (016) 932 4282
Fax: (016) 982 1050

THE SOUTH AFRICAN REINFORCED CONCRETE ENGINEERS ASSOCIATION (SARCEA)
PO Box 1338, Johannesburg 2000
Tel: (011) 834 6181
Fax: (011) 834 4792

CEMENT & CONCRETE INSTITUTE
Website: http://cnci.org.za/
Tel: (011) 315 0300
Fax: (011) 315 0584
E-mail: cnci@cnci.org.za
PO Box 168, Halfway House, 1685

ELECTRICAL CONTRACTORS ASSOCIATION (ECASA)
Website: http://www.ecasa.co.za/
Members: http://www.ecasa.co.za/
　Utilities/ToC.htm

HTH POOL ADVISORY SERVICE
Website: http://www.hth.co.za/
Toll-free: 0800 022 240
BLOEMFONTEIN
15 Fritz Stockenstroom Road, Oos-einde,
　Bloemfontein 9301
PO Box 282, Bloemfontein 9300
CAPE TOWN
2nd Floor, Sanclare Building, cnr Protea
　and Dreyer Street, Claremont 8000
PO Box 23245, Claremont 7735
Tel: (021) 617 140/1
Fax: (021) 619 344
GAUTENG
15 Spartan Crescent, Eastgate Ext 3,
　Sandton 2146
PO Box 114, Bergvlei 2012
Tel: (011) 444 2244

Fax: (011) 444 2240
NATAL
Suite 606, Overport City, Ridge Road,
 Durban 4001
Tel: (031) 209 0073
Fax: (031) 208 1261
PORT ELIZABETH
3rd Floor, Fedlife House, Ring Road,
 Green Acres 6045
PO Box 27151, Greenacres 6057
Tel: (041) 363 0188 or (041) 363 0205
Fax: (041) 363 0187
Export
15 Spartan Crescent, Eastgate Ext 3,
 Sandton 2146
PO Box 114, Bergvlei 2012
Tel: (011) 444 2244
Fax: (011) 444 2240
HTH® Customer Call Centre
15 Spartan Crescent, Eastgate Ext 3,
 Sandton 2146
PO Box 114, Bergvlei 2012
Tel: 0800 02 22 40
E-mail: poolassist@hth.co.za
Free pool water analysis performed at:
Kloopers, Bloemfontein
Tel: (051) 432 5513
Fax: (051) 432 4922

NATIONAL SPA AND POOL INSTITUTE OF SA
Website: http://www.nspi.co.za/
GAUTENG
Tel: (011) 791 1177
Fax: (011) 791 1483
PO Box 874, Randburg 2125
WESTERN CAPE
Tel: (021) 788 9141
Fax: (021) 788 9718
PO Box 39297, Capricorn Square 7948

SOUTH AFRICAN INTRUDER DETECTION SERVICES ASSOCIATION
Website: http://www.saidsa.co.za/
143 Newlands Avenue, Western Ext,
 Benoni 1501
Postal address: Postnet Suite #3 Private
 Bag X19, Gardenview 2047
Tel: (011) 845 4870/4828/4875
Fax: (011) 845 4850
E-mail: saidsa@mweb.co.za
Security associations website: http://www.
 security.co.za/associations.shtml

SOUTH AFRICAN NURSERYMEN'S ASSOCIATION(SANA)
PO Box 514, Halfway House 1685
Tel: (011) 464 1098
Fax: (011) 464 1099
E-mail: sana@iafrica.com
Website: www.sana.co.za

TIMBER FRAME BUILDERS ASSOCIATION
Website: http://www.tfba.co.za/
Tel: (021) 782 6596
Fax: (021) 782 6596
E-mail: secretary@tfba.co.za

SA WOOD PRESERVERS ASSOCIATION (SAWPA)
Private Bag X686, Isando 1600
Tel: (011) 974 1061
Fax: (011) 974 9779

EMERGENCY NUMBERS

EMERGENCY CONTROL CENTRE:

....

FIRE BRIGADE:

....

POLICE SERVICES:

....

....

POLICE FLYING SQUAD:

....

TRAFFIC DEPARTMENT:

....

....

AMBULANCE:

....

DOCTOR:

....

....

HOSPITALS:

....

....

POISON INFORMATION CENTRE:

....

....

SEA RESCUE (COASTAL AREAS):

....

MOUNTAIN RESCUE (CAPE):

....

VETERINARY SURGERY:

....

ANIMAL RESCUE ORGANISATIONS:

....

APIARIST (BEE SWARM REMOVAL):

....

HERPETOLOGIST (SNAKE REMOVAL):

....

....

OTHER:

....

....

USEFUL NUMBERS

ELECTRICIAN:

....

GARAGE:

....

LOCKSMITH:

....

MUNICIPAL OFFICES:

....

PLUMBER:

....

OTHER:

....

....